NICKY EPSTEIN
Crocheted Flowers

NICKY EPSTEIN

Crocheted Flowers

Nicky
Epstein
Books
An imprint of Sixth&Spring Books

Nicky Epstein Books

An imprint of Sixth&Spring Books
233 Spring Street, New York, New York 10013
sixthandspringbooks.com

Editorial Director
Elaine Silverstein

Book Division
Manager
Erica Smith

Associate Editor
Amanda Keiser

Art Directors
Chi Ling Moy
Diane Lamphron

Associate Art
Director
Sheena T. Paul

Graphic Designer
Michael Yong

Technical
Illustrations
Karen Manthey

Yarn Editor
Tanis Gray

Instructions Editor
Eve Ng

Instructions Checker
Jeannie Chin

Bookings Manager
Rachael Stein

Photography
Jennifer Lévy

Vice President,
Publisher
Trisha Malcolm

Production
Manager
David Joinnides

Creative Director
Joe Vior

President
Art Joinnides

Library of Congress Control Number: 2007921001
ISBN 10: 1-933027-95-9
ISBN 13: 978-1-933027-95-1

Manufactured in China
3   5   7   9   10   8   6   4   2

First Paperback Edition

This book is dedicated with love to my lifelong friend Jo Brandon, whose devotion, crochet expertise, and good humor have always been there for me.

I have always loved knitting flowers, whether as a motif for a full piece, an accent on a garment or bag, or to wear as a pin. The variety of colors and shapes of flowers appeals to me, and has continued to inspire my designs over the years. And yet, when I wrote my book *Knitted Flowers*, I was not sure of the reception it would get from critics and, more importantly, from knitters. After all, a book on just knitted flowers? Would people be interested? Would it have a wide appeal?

Well, I needn't have worried. The book took off like a rocket, with great reviews and widespread enthusiasm from knitters of all levels. It has become a mainstay in the libraries of thousands of knitters around the world.

It was then inevitable that my crochet friends would ask the question: "Hey, what about us?"

So here it is: *Crocheted Flowers*.

Crocheting is a wonderful medium to create all kinds of beautifully textured flowers. I'll show you how to crochet entire projects, create flower add-ons for original or purchased items like skirts, pillows, or even Chinese lanterns, and how to make flowers that stand on their own as a bouquet.

I'll also share with you some unique twists on creating crocheted flowers that I hope will help you think "outside the box" and inspire your own creativity. These flowers are quick and easy to make and are guaranteed to delight all who wear them or see them.

Enter into the beautiful crocheted flower garden and create a world of glorious color!

Nicky Epstein

table of contents

table of contents

stitch key

⬭ = chain (ch)
• = slip st (sl st)
✝ = single crochet (sc)
┬ = half double crochet (hdc)
┬ = double crochet (dc)
┬ = treble crochet (tr)
┬ = double treble crochet (dtr)

✕✕ = sc2tog
✕⋀✕ = sc3tog
⋀ = hdc2tog
— = work in back loop
— = work in front loop
⌄ = bullion st (wrap 5 times)
⌄ = bullion st (wrap 10 times)
= dc clusters

= tr clusters

= popcorns

abbreviations

Beg = begin(s)(ning)

Ch = chain

Dc = double crochet

Dc2tog = double crochet 2 together

Dtr = double triple crochet

Hdc = half double crochet

Hdc2tog = half double crochet 2 together

LH = left hand

Lp(s) = loop(s)

Rep = repeat

RH = right hand

Rnd (s) = round (s)

RS = right side

Sc = single crochet

Sc2tog = single crochet 2 together

Sc3tog = single crochet 3 together

Sl = slip

Sl st = slip stitch

Sp = space

St (s) = stitch(es)

Tr = triple crochet

WS = wrong side

Yo = yarn over

conversion chart

U.S. Term	U.K./AUS Term
sl st slip st	**sc** single crochet
sc single crochet	**dc** double crochet
hdc half double crochet	**htr** half treble crochet
dc double crochet	**tr** treble crochet
tr treble crochet	**dtr** double treble crochet
dtr double treble crochet	**trip tr** or **trtr** triple treble crochet
trtr triple treble crochet	**qtr** quadruple treble crochet
rev sc reverse single crochet	**rev dc** reverse double crochet
yo yarn over	**yoh** yarn over hook

chapter one layered petal flowers

The following flowers are made of individual crocheted petals; many are layered with another smaller flower as the center. Spoke, florette, and popcorn patterns can be used to center most of the flowers in the book. The fun thing is, petal flowers are interchangeable! Use the patterns in a variety of combinations to create your own floral masterpieces. Experimenting with different textured yarns and color combinations will also enhance the beauty of your flowers.

tatiana *and* rolfe

materials

1 2½oz/70g skein (each approx 168yds/154m) of Lion Brand Yarn *Microspun* (microfiber acrylic) in #102 blush (A) and #126 coffee (B)

Size F/5 (3.75mm) crochet hook

Tatiana

Petal (make 5)

With A, ch 11.

Row 1 (WS) Dc in 5th ch from hook, *ch 2, skip next 2 ch, 1 dc in next ch; rep from * to end—2 ch-2 sp made. Turn.

Rnd 2 Ch 1, 3 sc in first ch-2 sp, 3 sc in next ch-2 sp, 10 sc in end sp (working around to other side of foundation ch), [3 sc in next ch-2 sp] twice, 4 sc in sp made by end dc. Join with sl st to first sc.

Rnd 3 Working in back lps only, ch 1, [1 sc in next sc, ch 3, 1 sc in next sc (picot made)] 11 times, sl st in next sc—11 picots.

Fasten off.

Sew 5 petals together so they overlap at the base.

Spoke

With B, ch 5 and join with sl st in first ch to form a ring.

Rnd 1 Ch 1, 9 sc in ring.

Rnd 2 Working in a spiral through back lps only, 1 sc in each sc around.

Rnd 3 *Ch 7, 1 sc in 2nd ch from hook, 1 sl st in next 5 ch, 1 sc in next sc of rnd 2; rep from * around. Join with sl st in first ch of beg ch-7.

Fasten off.

tatiana

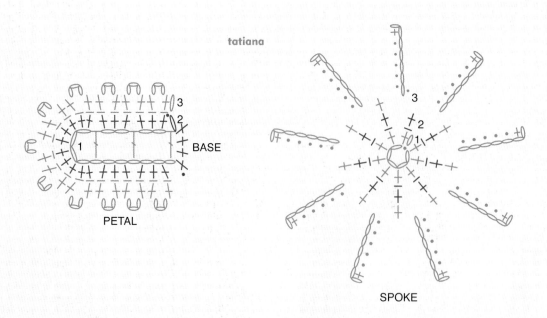

BASE

PETAL

SPOKE

tatiana

rolfe

Rolfe

Petal (make 5)

With B, ch 11.

Rnd 1 (RS) Sc in 2nd ch from hook, 1 sc in next 8 ch, 3 sc in last ch (working around to other side of foundation ch), 1 sc in next 8 ch, 2 sc in next ch—22 sc. Join with sl st to first sc.

Fasten off B and join A.

Rnd 2 (RS) With A, [ch 3, skip 2 sc, 1 sc in next sc] 3 times, [ch 3, skip 1 sc, 1 sc in next sc] twice, [ch 3, skip 2 sc,

1 sc in next sc] 3 times—8 ch-3 lps. Join with sl st to first ch of beg ch-3.

Fasten off.

Sew 5 petals together so they overlap at the base.

Florette

With A, ch 7 and join with sl st in first ch to form a ring.

Rnd 1 Ch 3, *1 sc in ring, ch 3; rep from * 3 times more. Join with sl st to first ch of beg ch-3.

Rnd 2 Ch 1, *[1 sc, 1 hdc, 1 dc, 2 tr, 1 dc,

1 hdc, 1 sc] in ch-3 sp; rep from * 4 times more. Join with sl st to first sc.

Fasten off.

rolfe

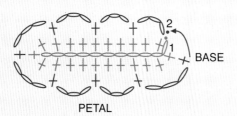

PETAL

FLORETTE

sunflower

materials

1 1¾oz/50g skein (each approx 122yd/110m) of GGH/Muench Yarns *Maxima*
(extafine superwash merino wool) in #5 gold (A), #10 brown (B) and #43 green (C)

Size D/3 (3.25mm) crochet hook

Size H/8 (5mm) crochet hook

Popcorn (pop) Work 4 dc in designated st, drop lp from hook, insert hook through top of first dc, pick up dropped lp and pull through.

Beg Popcorn (beg pop) Ch 3, work 3 dc in designated st(s), drop lp from hook, insert hook through top of first beg ch-3, pick up dropped lp and pull through.

With smaller hook and B, ch 2.

Rnd 1 10 sc in 2nd ch from hook. Join with sl st to first sc.

Rnd 2 *2 sc in next sc; rep from * to end—20 sc. Join with sl st to first sc.

Rnd 3 Work beg pop over next 3 sc, *ch 3, work pop over next 4 sc; rep from * around, end ch3—5 pops. Join with sl st to beg pop.

Rnd 4 Sl st in next ch-3 lp, beg pop in same ch-3 lp, ch 3, pop in next ch-3 lp, ch 3, pop in next pop, [ch 3, pop] in next 2 ch-3 lps, ch 3, pop in next pop, ch 3, pop in next ch-3 lp, end ch3—7 pops. Join with sl st to beg pop.

Rnd 5 Sl st in next ch-3 lp, beg pop in same ch-3 lp, *[ch 3, pop] in next ch-3 lp; rep from * around, end ch 3—7 pops. Join with sl st to beg pop.

Rnd 6 Ch 1, [sc in pop, 3 sc in next ch-3 lp] twice, sc in next pop, 4 sc in next ch-3 lp, sc in next pop, 3 sc in next ch-3 lp, sc in next pop, 4 sc in next ch-3 lp, [sc in next pop, 3 sc in next ch-3 lp] twice—30 sc. Join with sl st in first sc.

Fasten off B and join A.

Rnd 7 With A, ch 1, 1 sc in front lp of first sc, *ch 7, 1 sc in 4th ch from hook, 1 hdc in next ch, 1 dc in next ch, 1 tr in next ch, skip 2 sc of rnd 6, 1 sc in front lp of next sc; rep from * around, end last rep skip 2 sc of rnd 6—10 petals. Join with sl st to first sc.

Rnd 8 Working behind rnd 7, ch 1, 1 sc in back lp of next sc, *[ch 11, 1 sc in 4th ch from hook, 1 hdc in next ch, 1 dc in next ch, 1 tr in next 5 ch, skip 1 sc of rnd 6, **1 sc in back lp of next sc] twice, ch 11, 1 sc in 4th ch from hook, 1 hdc in next ch, 1 dc in next ch, 1 tr in next 5 ch, skip next 2 sc of rnd 6, 1 sc in in back lp of next sc; rep from * 3 times more, rep bet * to ** once—13 petals. Join with sl st to first sc.

Fasten off A.

Leaf

With larger hook and C, ch 15.

Rnd 1 Sl st in 2nd ch from hook, 1 sc in next ch, 1 hdc in next ch, 1 dc in next ch, 1 tr in next 6 ch, 1 dtr in next 4 ch, ch 1, 4 sc in side sp made by last dtr, sc in last ch, ch 4; working across other side of foundation ch, dtr in same ch, dtr in next 3 ch, tr in next 6 ch, 1 dc in next ch, 1 hdc, in next ch, 1 sc in next ch. Join with sl st in last ch.

Rnd 2 Sl st around to first dc, sl st in dc, [ch 1, sl st in tr] 6 times, [ch 1, sl st in dtr] 4 times, ch 1, sl st in next 5 sc, sl st in next 4 ch, [ch 1, sl st in next dtr] 4 times, [ch 1, sl st in next tr] 6 times, ch 1. Join with sl st to next dc.

Fasten off.

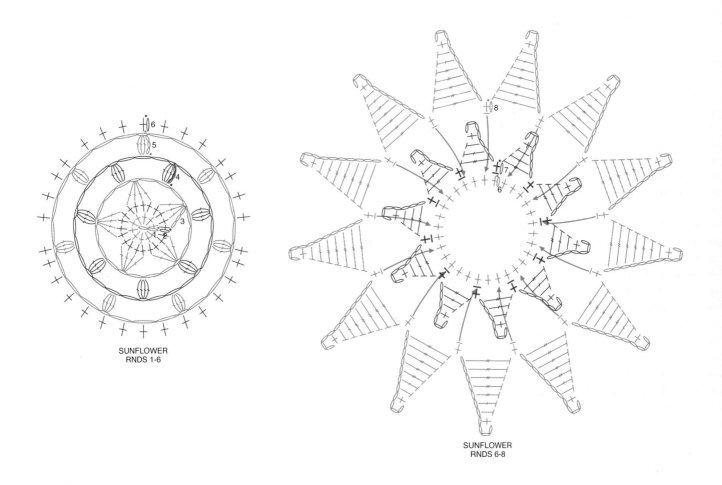

SUNFLOWER
RNDS 1-6

SUNFLOWER
RNDS 6-8

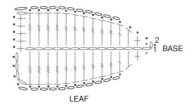

LEAF

poppy

materials

1 1¾oz/50g skein (each approx 61yd/55m) of Muench Yarns *Touch Me* (rayon microfiber/wool) in #3600 red (A), #3607 black (B) and #3633 olive (C)

Size C/2 (2.75mm) crochet hook

Petals

With A, ch 6. Join with sl st in first ch to form a ring.

Rnd 1 Ch 1, [1 sc in ring, ch 5] 5 times. Join with sl st to first sc—5 ch-sps.

Rnd 2 *Sl st in next ch-sp, [ch 4, 10 tr, ch 4, sl st] in same sp (petal made); rep from * 4 times more. Join with sl st to joining sl st—5 petals.

Rnd 3 *Sl st in next 4 ch along side of petal, ch 3, 1 dc in next 10 tr, ch 3, sl st in next 4 ch down side of petal; rep from * 4 times more. Join with sl st to first sl st.

Fasten off, leaving a long tail.

Center

With B, ch 2.

Rnd 1 6 sc in 2nd ch from hook. Join with sl st to first sc.

Rnd 2 Ch 1, 2 sc in same sc and in each sc to end. Join with sl st to first sc—12 sc.

Rnd 3 Ch 4, 1 tr in same sc, 2 tr in each sc to end. Join with sl st to top of beg ch.

Fasten off, leaving a long tail.

Position Center behind Petals, tucking the middle out through center opening of petals. Sew in place using tails.

Leaf

With smaller hook and C, ch 6.

Stem row 1 sc in 2nd ch from hook and in each ch to end—5 sc.

Row 1 Working into side of last sc, ch 1, 3 sc in end st. Ch 1, turn.

Row 2 2 sc in first sc, 1 sc in next sc, 2 sc in last sc—5 sc. Ch 1, turn.

Rows 3, 5, 7 and 9 1 sc in each sc to end. Ch 1, turn.

Row 4 1 sc in first sc, 2 sc in next sc, 1 sc in next sc, 2 sc in next sc, 1 sc in last sc—7 sc. Ch 1, turn.

Row 6 1 sc in first sc, [sc2tog, 1 sc in next sc] twice—5 sc. Ch 1, turn.

Row 8 Sc2tog, 1 sc in next sc, sc2tog—3 sts. Ch 1, turn.

Row 10 Sc3tog.

Fasten off.

PETALS

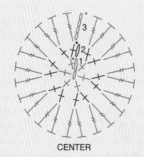

CENTER

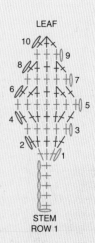

LEAF

STEM
ROW 1

daisy mays

materials

1 1¾oz/50g hank (each approx 108yd/97m) of Tahki Yarns/Tahki•Stacy Charles, Inc. *Cotton Classic* (mercerized cotton) in #3549 maize, #3725 green, #3358 terra cotta, #3488 red, and #3712 sage

Size F/5 (3.75mm) crochet hook

Note

Colors for flowers, centers and leaves can be combined interchangeably. (Sized for small flower, with large flower in parentheses.)

Small Flower

Ch 5 (10). Join with sl st in first ch to form a ring.

Rnd 1 Ch 1, 12 (24) sc in ring. Join with sl st to first sc.

Rnd 2 *Ch 7 (14), 1 sc in 2nd ch from hook and in each ch to end (petal made), 1 sc in next 2 sc of ring; rep from * around—6 (12) petals. Join with sl st to first ch of beg ch—7 (14).

Rnd 3 *1 Sc in each foundation ch along side of next petal to last ch, 5 sc in last ch (working around to other side of petal), 1 sc in each sc along side of petal, skip next sc of ring, 1 sc in next sc; rep from * for each petal. Join with sl st to first sc.

Fasten off.

Center

Ch 2.

Rnd 1 5 sc in 2nd ch from hook.

Rnd 2 Working in a spiral in back lps only, 2 sc in each st to end—10 sc.

Rnd 3 *1 Sc in next st, 2 sc in next st; rep from * to end—15 sc.

For Small Center Join with sl st to first sc.

For Large Center Rep rnd 3, end 1 sc in last st—22 sc. Join with sl st to first sc.

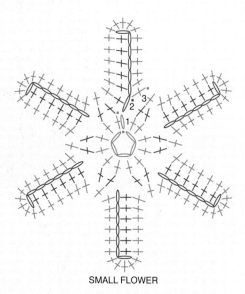

SMALL FLOWER

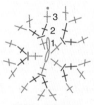

SMALL CENTER

daisy mays

cont. from previous page

Fasten off, leaving a long tail. Stuff center with scrap yarn, then thread tail through top edge of last rnd and pull tightly to gather. Fasten securely. Sew to center of flower.

Leaves

Ch 10. Join with sl st in first ch to form a ring.

Rnd 1 Ch 1, 24 sc in ring. Join with sl st to first sc.

Row 2 Ch 15, 1 sc in 2nd ch from hook, 1 hdc in next ch, 1 dc in next ch, 1 tr in next 8 ch, 1 dc in next ch, 1 hdc in next ch, 1 sc in next ch (leaf made), sl st in next sc of ring. Turn.

Row 3 Ch 1, 1 sc in each st along side of leaf, 3 sc in end ch of last st (working around to other side of petal), 1 sc in each foundation ch along side of leaf, sl st in next sc of ring. Turn.

Row 4 Working in back lps only across RH side of leaf, ch 1, 1 sc in each st along side of leaf to center of 3-sc group, 3 sc in center st, 1 sc in each st along side of leaf, sl st in next sc of ring.

For second leaf, 1 sc in next 2 sc of ring and rep rows 1–4.

Fasten off. Position leaves behind flower as desired and sew in place.

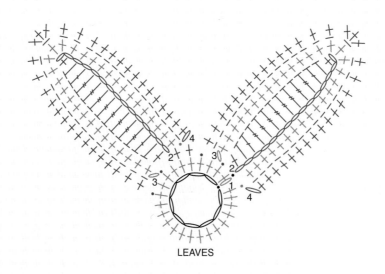

LEAVES

3
2
1

LARGE FLOWER

4
3
2
1

LARGE CENTER

holiday beauty

materials

1 1¾oz/50g skein (each approx 61yd/55m) of Muench Yarns *Touch Me* (rayon microfiber/wool) in #3600 red (A), #3620 dark red (B) and #3648 light green (C)

1 1¾oz/50g skein (each approx 61yd/55m) of Muench Yarns *Touch Me Due* (rayon microfiber/wool) in #5404 (D) green mix

Size C/2 (2.75mm) crochet hook

Center

With B, ch 15.

Row 1 2 Tr in 4th ch from hook, *3 tr in next ch; rep from * to end. Turn.

Row 2 *Ch 5, 1 sc in next st; rep from *, end last rep 1 sc in top of beg ch.

Fasten off.

Roll chain edge so piece spirals in on itself and sew in place.

Petals (make 5)

With A, ch 4. Join with sl st in first ch to form a ring.

Row 1 Ch 1, [1 sc, 1 hdc, 1 dc, 1 tr, 3 dtr, 1 tr, 1 dc, 1 hdc, 1 sc] in ring. Ch 1, turn.

Row 2 1 Sc in each st to end. Ch 1, turn.

Row 3 *1 Sc in next 2 sc, 2 sc in next sc; rep from *, end 1 sc in last 2 sc.

Fasten off.

Base

With A, ch 4. Join with sl st in first ch to form a ring.

Rnd 1 Ch 3 (counts as 1 dc), 11 dc in ring—12 dc.

Rnd 2 Working in a spiral, 2 dc in each dc around—24 dc.

Rnd 3 *1 dc in next dc, 2 dc in next dc; rep from * around—36 dc. Join with sl st to first dc.

Fasten off.

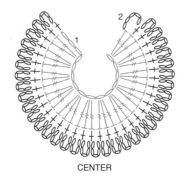

CENTER

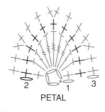

PETAL

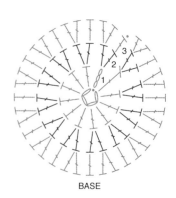

BASE

Place flat edge of petals evenly around edge of base and sew in place. Position center over base and sew in place.

Berries (make 5)

With C, ch 4. Join with sl st in first ch to form a ring.

Rnd 1 Ch 2, 10 dc in ring. Join with sl st to top of beg ch-2.

Fasten off leaving a long tail. Thread tail though tops of dcs, pull tightly and fasten securely. Using tails, make chains to join.

Leaf (make 3)

With D, ch 14.

Rnd 1 Sl st in 2nd ch from hook, 1 sc in next 3 ch, 1 hdc in next 2 ch, 1 dc in next 3 ch, 2 hdc in next 2 ch, 1 sc in next ch, 3 sc in last ch (working around to other side of foundation ch), 1 sc in next ch, 1 hdc in next 2 ch, 1 dc in next 3 ch, 1 hdc in next 2 ch, 1 sc in next 3 ch, sl st in next ch.

Rnd 2 Working in back loops only, ch 1, sl st in each st to center st of 3-sc group, ch 3, skip center st, sl st in each st to end.

Fasten off, leaving a long tail.

Center ridge With RS facing and using tail, embroider 1 chain st for each ch along foundation ch. Ch 4 for stem. Fasten off.

Position leaves and berries as desired and sew in place.

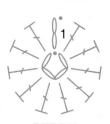

BERRY

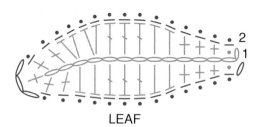

LEAF

baroque bloom *and* starlight double star

materials

1 1¾oz/50g ball (each approx 113yds/102m) of Muench Yarns *Verikeri*
(nylon/polyester) in #4111 green (A), #4114 dark green (B) and #4108 teal (C)

Size F/5 (3.75mm) crochet hook

Size C/2 (2.75mm) crochet hook for smaller star only

Store-bought decorative buttons

Baroque Bloom

Bottom layer

With A, ch 3. Join with sl st in first ch to form a ring.

Rnd 1 Ch 3 (counts as 1 dc), 9 dc in ring. Join with sl st to top of beg ch.

Rnd 2 Ch 1, *1 sc in next st, 2 sc in next st; rep from * around—15 sc. Join with sl st to first sc.

Fasten off A and join B.

Rnd 3 *Ch 11, sl st in 2nd ch from hook, 1 sc in next ch, 1 hdc in next ch, 1 dc in next 4 ch, 1 tr in next 3 ch, skip next 2 sc of ring, sl st in front lp of next sc of rnd 2; rep from * around—5 petals.

Fasten off B and join A.

Rnd 4 *Working along foundation ch of petal, ch 1, 1 sc in each ch to last ch, 3 sc in last ch (working around tip), 1 sc in each st to base of petal, sc2tog skipped sts of ring; rep from * around. Fasten off.

Middle layer

With A, ch 10. Join with sl st in first ch to form a ring.

Rnd 1 *Ch 11, sl st in 2nd ch from hook, 1 sc in next ch, 1 hdc in next ch, 1 dc in next 3 ch, 1 tr in next 4 ch, skip 1 ch of ring, sl st in next ch; rep from * around—5 petals.

Fasten off A and join B.

Rnd 2 *Working along foundation ch of petal, ch 1, 1 sc in each ch to last ch, 3 sc in last ch (working around tip), 1 sc in each st to base of petal, sc2tog skipped sts of ring; rep from * around. Join with sl st to first sc. Fasten off.

Top layer

With A, ch 3. Join with sl st in first ch to form a ring.

Rnd 1 Ch 1, 8 sc in ring. Join with sl st to first sc.

Rnd 2 *Ch 6, 1 dc in 3rd ch from hook and in next 3 ch, skip 1 st of ring, sl st in next st; rep from * around—4 petals.

Fasten off.

Arrange layers so petals alternate and sew in place. If desired, sew decorative button at center.

baroque bloom

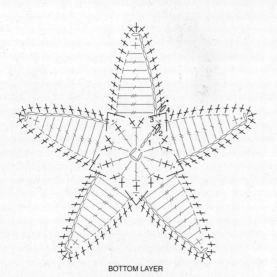

BOTTOM LAYER

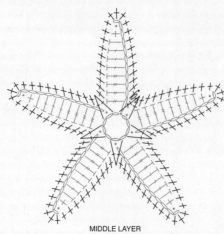

MIDDLE LAYER

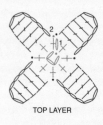

TOP LAYER

Starlight Double Star

CL2 (2-dc cluster) [Yo and draw up lp, yo and draw through 2 lps] twice in same sp, yo and draw through all 3 lps.

Small star

Using C and smaller hook, ch 2.

Rnd 1 5 sc in 2nd ch from hook. Join with sl st to first sc..

Rnd 2 Ch 1, *3 sc in next sc; rep from * around. Join with sl st to first sc—15 sc.

Rnd 3 Ch 1, *1 sc in next sc, ch 6, sl st in 2nd ch from hook, 1 sc in next ch, 1 hdc in next ch, 1 dc in next ch, 1 tr in next ch, 1 tr in base of same sc of ring, skip next 2 sc; rep from * 4 times more. Join with sl st to first sc—5 points.

Fasten off.

Large star

Using C and larger hook, ch 5. Join with sl st in first ch to form a ring.

Rnd 1 Ch 2, 1 dc in ring (beg cluster), ch 4, *CL2 in ring, ch 4; rep from * 3 times more. Join with sl st to top of beg cluster—5 clusters.

Rnd 2 Ch 1, *1 sc in top of cluster, ch 7, 1 sc in 4th ch from hook, 1 hdc in next ch, 1 dc in next ch, 1 tr in last ch; rep from * 4 times more. Join with sl st to first sc—5 points.

Fasten off.

Place small star on top of large star so points alternate, sew in place. If desired, sew decorative button at center.

starlight double star

SMALL STAR

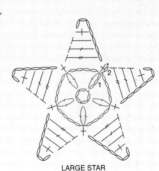

LARGE STAR

jardin du luxembourg

french florettes • lady finger lace • luxembourg flower

materials

1 ⅙oz/5g hank (each approx 16yd/15m) of DMC 3 Coton Perlé in #3687 rose (A), #601 lt pink (B), 605 dk pink (C) and 444 yellow (D)

Size F/5 (3.75mm) crochet hook

French Florettes

Small florette

CL2 (2-dc cluster) [Yo and draw up lp, yo and draw through 2 lps] twice in same sp, yo and draw through all 3 lps.

With B, ch 4.

Rnd 1 CL2 in 4th ch from hook, ch 3, sl st in same ch, *[ch 3, CL2, ch 3, sl st] in same ch*; rep from * 3 times more— 5 petals.

For a string of florettes, *ch 9 and rep rnd 1; rep from * for desired number of florettes. Fasten off.

Large florette

CL2 (2-tr cluster) [Yo twice and draw up lp, (yo and draw through 2 lps) twice] twice in same sp, yo and draw through all 3 lps.

With B, ch 5.

Rnd 1 CL2 in 5th ch from hook, ch 4, sl st in same ch, *[ch 4, CL2, ch 4, sl st] in same ch*; rep from * 3 times more— 5 petals.

For a string of florettes, *ch 10 and rep rnd 1; rep from * for desired number of florettes. Fasten off.

Lady Finger Lace

Petals

With B, ch 5. Join with sl st in first ch to form a ring.

Rnd 1 Ch 1, 8 sc in ring. Join with sl st to first sc.

Rnd 2 Ch 1, 2 sc in each sc to end. Join with sl st to first sc—16 sc.

Row 3 Ch 12, 1 sc in 2nd ch from hook, *ch 1, skip 1 ch, 1 sc in next ch; rep from * 4 times more, sl st in next sc of ring (petal made). Turn.

french florettes

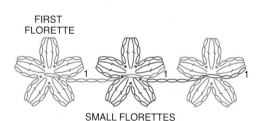

SMALL FLORETTES

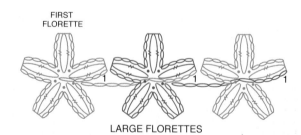

LARGE FLORETTES

french florettes

lady finger lace

luxembourg flower

jardin du luxembourg

cont. from previous page

Row 4 Working on petal, ch 1, 1 sc in first ch-1 sp, *ch 1, 1 dc in next ch-1 sp; rep from * 3 times more, ch 1, 1 sc in last sc. Turn.

Row 5 Ch 1, 1 sc in first ch-1 sp, *ch 1, 1 dc in next ch-1 sp; rep from * 3 times more, ch 1, 1 sc in last sc, sl st in next sc of ring. Turn.

Row 6 Rep row 4.

Row 7 *Ch 1, 1 sc in next ch-1 sp; rep from * 4 times more, 1 sc in last sc, sl st in next sc of ring.

Rep rows 3-7 four times more—5 petals. Fasten off.

Center

With D, ch 5. Join with sl st in first ch to form a ring.

Rnd 1 Ch 1, 7 sc in ring. Join with sl st to first sc.

Rnd 2 *Ch 8, 1 sc in 2nd ch from hook and in each ch across, sl st in next sc of ring; rep from * around.

Fasten off.

You can vary the lengths of the stamens by increasing or decreasing the number of chains at the beginning of rnd 2.

Place at center of flower and sew in place.

lady finger lace

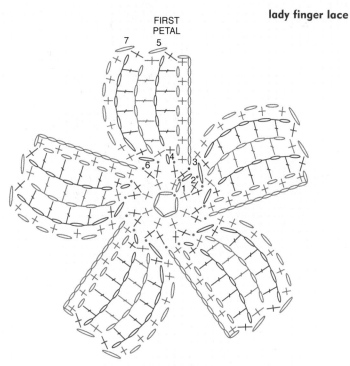

FIRST PETAL

7   5

6   4   3
2
1

PETALS

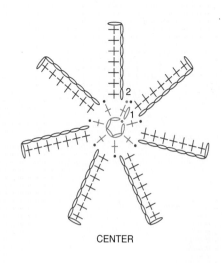

2
1

CENTER

Luxembourg Flower

Outer petals

With C, ch 5. Join with sl st in first ch to form a ring.

Rnd 1 Ch 1, 6 sc in ring. Join with sl st to first sc.

Rnd 2 Ch 1, 2 sc in each sc around. Join with sl st to first sc—12 sc.

Rnd 3 Rep Rnd 2—24 sc.

Rnd 4 Working in front lps only, *ch 3, 1 tr in same sp, 2 tr in next 2 sc, 1 tr in next sc, ch 3, sl st in same space, sl st in next sc; rep from * 5 times more - 6 petals. Fasten off.

Inner petals

With B, ch 5. Join with sl st in first ch to form a ring.

Rnd 1 *Ch 3, 2 tr in ring, ch 3, sl st in ring; rep from * 4 times more—5 petals. Fasten off.

Center

Make same as for Lady Finger Lace.

Place Inner petals over Outer petals and Center over Inner petals. Sew in place.

luxembourg flower

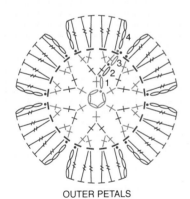

OUTER PETALS

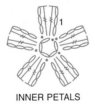

INNER PETALS

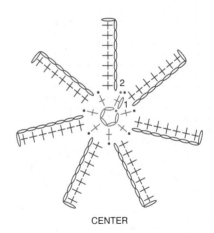

CENTER

earflap hat

one size

Approx 20"/51cm diam

gauge

7 sts = 4" in single crochet with B, C and D held tog using larger hook

materials

1 .70oz/20g ball (approx 90yd/82m) of Trendsetter Yarns *Charm* (polyamide/tactel nylon) in #4412 hawaiian punch (A)

1 1¾oz/50g ball (approx 80yd/73m) of Trendsetter Yarns *Dune* (mohair/nylon/acrylic) in #119 purple/purple (B) and #117 red/red (C)

1 1¾oz/50g ball (approx 100yd/91m) of Lane Borgosesia/Trendsetter Yarns *Merino Otto* (wool) in #60 red (D)

Sizes H/8 and N/13 (5 and 9mm) crochet hooks

Assorted beads (optional)

With larger hook and B, C and D held tog, ch 2.

Rnd 1 5 sc in 2nd ch from hook. Join with sl st to first sc.

Rnds 2 and 4 Ch 1, 2 sc in each sc around—20 sc after rnd 3. Join with sl st to first sc.

Rnd 3 Ch 1, 1 sc in each sc around. Join with sl st to first sc.

Rnd 5 Ch 1, *1 sc in next sc, 2 sc in next sc; rep from * around—30 sc. Join with sl st to first sc.

Rnd 6 Ch 3, 1 dc next sc and in each sc around—30 dc. Join with sl st in top of beg ch.

Rnd 7 Ch 3, 1 dc in next 4 dc, 2 dc in next dc, *1 dc in next 5 dc, 2 dc in next dc; rep from * around—35 dc. Join with sl st in top of beg ch.

Rnds 8 and 9 Ch 3, 1 dc in next dc and in each dc around. Join with sl st in top of beg ch.

Fasten off B and C, and join A.

Rnd 10 With smaller hook and A and D held tog, ch 3 (counts as 1 dc), *2 dc in next dc, 1 dc in next dc; rep from * around—52 dc. Join with sl st in top of beg ch.

Rnds 11 and 12 Ch 3, 1 dc in next dc and in each dc around. Join with sl st in top of beg ch.

earflap hat

cont. from previous page

Rnds 13 and 14 Ch 1, 1 sc in each st around. Join with sl st to first sc.

Fasten off.

Earflaps

Place markers along edge of hat for earflaps.

With RS facing, join A and D at marker.

Row 1 Ch 1, 1 sc in next 7 sts. Turn.

Row 2 Ch 2, 1 dc in each sc. Turn.

Row 3 Ch 2, skip 1 dc, 1 dc in next 3 dc, dc2tog—5 dc. Turn.

Row 4 Ch 2, skip 1 dc, 1 dc in next dc, dc2tog—3 dc. Turn.

Row 5 Ch 2, dc2tog.

Fasten off.

Repeat on opposite side for 2nd earflap.

Tie cords (make 2)

With smaller hook and A and D held tog, ch 4. Join with sl st in first ch to form a ring.

Row 1 Ch 1, 1 sc in each ch around—4 sc. Join with sl st to first sc.

Row 2 Ch 1, 1 sc in each sc around. Join with sl st to first sc.

Rep row 2 for 12"/30.5cm or to desired length.

Fasten off, leaving a 6"/15cm tail for sewing.

Embellishments

Small flowers

(Make 9 as foll: 3 B and 6 C)

With smaller hook, ch 6.

Rnd 1 In 6th ch from hook, [1 dc, ch 2] 7 times—8 posts. Join with sl st in 4th ch of beg ch-6.

Rnd 2 Ch 1, [1 sc, ch 1, 2 dc, ch 1, 1 sc] in each ch-2 sp around. Join with sl st to first sc.

Rnd 3 Working in front of rnd 2, *sl st around front post of next dc of rnd 1, ch 6; rep from * around. Join with sl st in first sl st.

Fasten off.

Large flowers (make 2 with B and C held tog)

With larger hook, ch 6.

Rnds 1 and 2 Work same as small flower.

Fasten off B and C. Join A in any st of rnd 2.

Rnd 3 Ch 1, sc in each st and ch-sp around. Join with sl st to first sc.

Fasten off.

Finishing

Join A in any st at back edge of hat. Ch 1, sc evenly around front and back edges and earflaps. Join with sl st in first sc. Fasten off.

For each earflap, place small B flower over large flower and sew in place. Embellish centers with beads if desired. Place 2 small C flowers across back edge of hat between earflaps and sew in place. Place a small C flower at each side of front edge between earflaps and sew in place. Place small B flower at center and sew in place. Sew one tie cord to end of each earflap, then sew a small C flower to each end of tie cord.

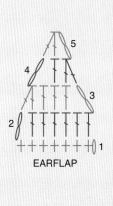

EARFLAP

SMALL FLOWER

LARGE FLOWER

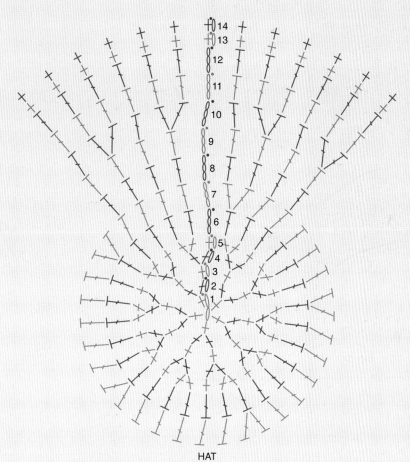

HAT

fiesta flower handbag

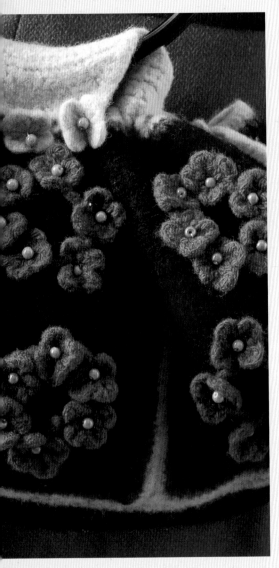

size

Approx 18"W x 11"H after felting

gauge

14¾ sts x 11 rws=4"/10cm in dc st after felting, using size G/6 (4mm) crochet hook

materials

2 1¾oz/50g skeins (each approx 110yd/99m) of Classic Elite Yarns *Renaissance* (wool) in #7113 black (A)

1 skein each #7135 celery (B), #7178 tiled roof (C) and #7124 giotto grape (D)

Size G/6 (4mm) crochet hook

42 green 6mm round beads

50 gold 6mm round beads

1 magnetic snap

1 pr 8½"/21.5cm round plastic handles

Flowers

Make 14 small French Florettes (see page 32): 7 each with C and D.

For each flower chain, make 6 flowers working ch 4 between flowers. Form flower rings by ending flower chain with ch 4, join with sl st to base of first CL2 of first flower. Set aside to attach to finished purse.

Handbag

Front and back panels (make 6)

With A, Ch 27.

Row 1 1 Dc in 4th ch from hook and in each ch to end—25 dc. Turn.

Row 2 Ch 2 (counts as 1 dc), 1 dc in each dc across—25 dc. Turn.

Rep row 2 until there are 21 rows.

Fasten off.

Edging

Join C at top right corner of panel.

Rnd 1 With C, ch 1, 3 sc in first dc, 1 sc in each sc to last sc, 3 sc in last sc; working along side edge, 2 sc in side of next 21 dc; working along foundation ch,

fiesta flower handbag

cont. from previous page

3 sc in first ch, 1 sc in each ch to last ch, 3 sc in last ch; working along rem side edge, 2 sc in side of next 21 dc—152 sc. Join with sl st to first sc.

Fasten off C, join B.

Rnd 2 With B, ch 1, 1 sc in first sc, 3 sc in next sc, *1 sc in each sc to next 3-sc group, 1 sc in next sc, 3 sc in next sc; rep from * twice more, 1 sc in each sc to end—160 sc. Join with sl st to first sc.

Fasten off.

Work 5 more panels as for first panel. Join panels by placing RS tog and sl st tog along one side seam with B.

Drawstring casing and handle flap

With WS facing, join B to top edge of front.

Row 1 Ch 1, 83 sc evenly across. Turn

Row 2 Ch 3 (counts as 1 dc), skip 3 sc, 1 dc in next sc, *skip 1 sc, 1 dc in next sc; rep from * to last 4 sc, skip 3 sc, 1 dc in last sc—40 dc. Turn.

Row 3 Ch 1, 1 sc in each dc across—40 sc. Turn.

Rows 4 and 5 Ch 1, skip next sc, 1 sc in each sc to last 2 sc, skip next sc, 1 sc in last sc—36 sc after row 5. Turn.

Rows 6-10 Ch 1, [sc2tog] twice, 1 sc in next sc and in each sc to last 4 sc, [sc2tog] twice—16 sc after row 10. Turn.

Row 11 *Ch 9, make French Florette, 1 sc in each ch of beg ch-9, 1 sc in next 7 sc of row 10; rep from * twice more, end last rep 1 sc in last sc of row 10—3 flowers.

Fasten off.

Repeat for back of purse.

Gusset panel

With A, ch 14.

Row 1 1 dc in 4th ch from hook and in each ch across—12 dc. Turn.

Row 2 Ch 3, 1 dc in each dc across—12 dc. Turn.

Rep row 2 until there are 82 rows.

Fasten off.

Top edging

With RS facing, join C to top right edge of gusset panel.

Ch 1, 1 sc in each dc across—12 sc.

Fasten off. Rep at other end of panel.

Side pocket

With A, ch 12.

Row 1 1 sc in 2nd ch from hook and in each ch across—11 sc. Turn.

Row 2 Ch 1, 1 sc in each sc across—11 sc. Turn.

Rep row 2 until there are 22 rows.

Fasten off.

Gusset edging and pocket join

Position side pocket with its top edge approx 4½"/11.5cm below top edge of gusset panel and pin in place. With RS facing, join B to top right edge of gusset panel.

Row 1 Ch 1, 3 sc in same st, 1 sc in each sc to last sc, 3 sc in last sc; working along side edge of panel, 2 sc in side of each dc to end and sc through both layers to join pocket; 3 sc in next sc of opposite top edge, 1 sc in each sc to last sc, 3 sc in last sc; working along other side edge of panel, 2 sc in side of each dc to end and sc through both layers to join other side of pocket. Join with sl st to first sc.

Fasten off.

Pocket flap

Join B above top edge of pocket, pick up and sc 12 sts across dc row of gusset panel. Turn.

Rows 1 and 2 Ch 1, 1 sc in each sc across—12 sc. Turn.

Row 3 Ch 1, 1 sc in next 6 sc, ch 9, make French Florette, 1 sc in each ch of ch-9, 1 sc in next 6 sc.

Fasten off.

With RS tog, pin gusset panel to front and back edges of purse. Join panels by sl st tog along both side seams with B.

Drawstring

With B, make one French Florette, ch 175, turn 1 sc in each ch of ch-175. Fasten off. Make a second florette to finish end after felting.

Finishing

Weave in ends. Place handbag, drawstrings and florettes into a laundry bag and felt (see p.144).

With sewing needle and thread, sew beads to flower centers and sew flower rings to handbag as pictured or where desired. Attach magnetic clasp above drawstring casing. Fold handle flaps to RS of handbag, enclosing one handle on each side and sew securely in place using matching yarn. Lace drawstring through casing row on both front and back and sew florette to ends.

chapter two

one-piece flowers

Although these classic beauties look complicated, they are all easy to make. As you crochet, they form beautiful shapes before your eyes. These flowers look wonderful when applied to crocheted garments. The floral necklette on page 64 is a lovely example of how to use these flowers in combination.

There are a variety of beautiful beaded yarns that can be used to crochet flowers. Wonderful beads, buttons and fringes are also available to enhance the centers of the flowers.

pansy party

materials

1 1¾oz/50g skein (each approx 61yd/55m) of Muench Yarns *Touch Me* (rayon microfiber/wool) in #3632 gold, #3650 lt yellow, #3626 lt blue, #3627 dk blue, #3645 lt orchid, #3602 purple, #3643 lavender

Size C/2 (2.75mm) crochet hook

Version I #3650 lt yellow (A), #3626 lt blue (B), #3627 dk blue (C)

Version II #3632 gold (A), #3645 lt orchid (B), #3602 purple (C)

Version III #3650 lt yellow (A), #3643 lavender (B), #3602 purple (C)

With A, ch 2.

Rnd 1 Work 5 sc in 2nd ch from hook, join with sl st in first sc.

Fasten off A and join B.

Rnd 2 Ch 1, 2 sc in same sc, [ch 6, 2 sc in next sc] 4 times, ch 6, sl st in first sc—5 ch-sp.

Drop B and join C.

Rnd 3 *Sl st in next ch-sp, [sc, hdc, dc, ch 1, (tr, ch 1) 10 times, dc, hdc, sc] in same sp; rep from * once more. Pick up B, **sl st in next ch-sp, [sc, hdc, 8 dc, hdc, sc] in same sp; rep from ** twice more, join with sl st in first sl st—2 large petals and 3 small petals.

Fasten off C and pick up B.

Rnd 4 *Sc in each of next 3 sts, sc in each of next 11 ch-1 sps, sc in each of next 3 sts; rep from * once across 2nd large petal.

Fasten off.

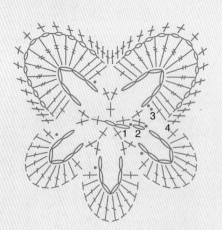

narcisse

materials

1 3½oz/100g skein (approx 205yd/187m) of Lorna's Laces *Lion and Lamb* (silk/wool) in #64 gold hill

Size G/6 (4mm) crochet hook

Outer petals

With A, ch 10. Join with sl st in first ch to form a ring.

Rnd 1 Ch 1, [1 sc, 1 hdc, 3 dc, 1 hdc, 1 sc, sl st] 5 times in ring—5 petals. Join with sl st to first sc.

Rnd 2 *10 sc evenly spaced around next petal, sl st between petals; rep from * around.

Rnd 3 *Ch 4, sl st between petals; rep from * around.

Fasten off.

Corona

Join B between any 2 petals.

Rnd 1 *[2 sc, ch 2, 2 sc] in ch-4 sp; rep from * around. Join with sl st to first sc.

Fasten off.

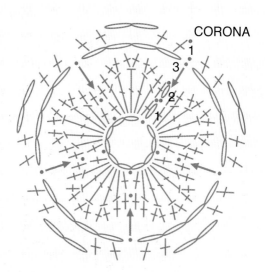

CORONA

poinsettia with beads

materials

1 1¾oz/50g spool (approx 145yd/133m) of Fonty/Russi Sales *Serpentine* (nylon) in #846 tomato

2.5mm beads

Size C/2 (2.75mm) crochet hook

String approx 50 beads onto silk. Slide beads up to hook and work randomly into sts, pulling beads to RS of work.

Center

Ch 5. Join with sl st in first ch to form a ring.

Rnd 1 Ch 1, [1 sc, ch 4] 8 times in ring. Join with sl st to first sc.

Rnd 2 Working behind rnd 1 lps, ch 2, [sl st in next sc, ch 2] 7 times. Join with sl st in beg ch. Do not cut yarn.

Petals

Row 1 Sl st in next ch-2 sp, [ch 1, 4 sc] in same sp. Ch 1, turn.

Row 2 2 sc in first sc, 1 sc in next 2 sc, 2 sc in last sc—6 sc. Ch 1, turn.

Rows 3 and 4 1 Sc in each sc to end. Ch 1, turn.

Rows 5, 6, 7 and 8 Sc2tog, 1 sc in each sc to end. Ch 1, turn.

Row 9 Sc2tog, sl st along side of petal to base, sl st in same ch-2 sp.

Rep rows 1–9 seven times more—8 petals.

Fasten off.

FIRST PETAL

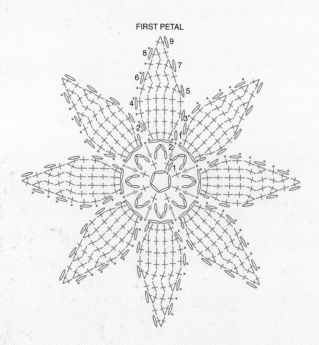

beaded irish rose

materials

1 .35oz/10g ball (each approx 45yd/41m) of Presencia *Finca No 5* (cotton) in #C/8327 taupe, #C/5229 olive or #C8083 black

Size F/5 (3.75mm) crochet hook

3mm or 3.5mm beads (make sure hole is large enough to fit on thread)

7mm rhinestone for center

SB (slide bead) Slide bead to work.

Ch 5. Join with sl st in first ch to form a ring.

Rnd 1 Ch 6, [1 dc, ch 3] 7 times in ring. Join with sl st in 3rd ch of beg ch—8 ch-sp.

Rnd 2 Ch 1, *[1 sc, 1 hdc, 1 dc, SB, 2 dc, 1 hdc, 1 sc] in ch-3 sp; rep from * 7 times more. Join with sl st to first sc.

Rnd 3 Ch 6, [1 dc in back of rnd 1 dc, ch 3] 7 times. Join with sl st in 3rd ch of beg ch.

Rnd 4 Ch 1, *[1 sc, 1 hdc, 1 dc, SB, 2 dc, 1 hdc, 1 sc] in ch-3 sp; rep from * 7 times more. Join with sl st to first sc.

Rnd 5 Working behind rnd 2, sl st in first sl st of rnd 1, ch 5, [sl st in next dc of rnd 1, ch 5] 7 times. Join with sl st to first sl st.

Rnd 6 Ch 1, *[1 sc, 1 hdc, 2 dc, SB, 3 dc, 1 hdc, 1 sc] in ch-5 sp; rep from * 7 times more. Join with sl st to first sc.

Rnd 7 Working behind rnd 4, sl st in first sl st of rnd 3, ch 7, [sl st in next dc of rnd 3, ch 7] 7 times. Join with sl st to first sl st.

Rnd 8 Ch 1, *[1 sc, 1 hdc, 3 dc, SB, 4 dc, 1 hdc, 1 sc] in ch-7 sp; rep from * 7 times more. Join with sl st to first sc.

Fasten off.

Attach rhinestone to center.

bluebell and *belle flores*

materials (bluebell)

1 ⅒oz/5g hank (approx 16yd/15m) of DMC 3 *Coton Perlé* in #341 lt blue

Size C/2 (2.75mm) crochet hook

8mm round beads

materials (belle flores)

1 ¾oz/50g ball (approx 200yd/182m) of Bernat *Cool Crochet* (cotton/nylon) in #74130 blues

Size F/5 (3.75mm) crochet hook

Bluebell

Ch 4, leaving a 2½"/5.5cm tail. Join with sl st in first ch to form a ring.

Rnd 1 Ch 1, 8 sc in ring. Join with sl st to first sc—8 sc.

Rnds 2, 3 and 4 Ch 1, 1 sc in each sc around. Join with sl st to first sc.

Rnd 5 Ch 1, 2 sc in each sc around. Join with sl st to first sc—16 sc.

Rnd 6 Ch 1, *1 sc in next st, 1 dc in next st, 3 tr in next st, 1 dc in next st; rep from * around. Join with sl st in first sc.

Fasten off.

Sew bead to center of flower.

Belle Flores

Ch 4. Join with sl st in first ch to form a ring.

Rnd 1 Ch 1, 9 sc in ring. Join with sl st to first sc.

Rnd 2 Ch 1, 1 sc in each sc around. Join with sl st to first sc—9 sc.

Rnd 3 Ch 1, 2 sc in each sc around. Join with sl st to first sc—18 sc.

Rnds 4, 5 and 6 Ch 1, 1 sc in each sc around. Join with sl st to first sc.

Rnd 7 Ch 3 (counts as 1 tr), 1 tr in same st, 2 tr in each sc around. Join with sl st to top of beg ch—36 tr.

Rnd 8 *Ch 2, 1 sc in 2nd ch from hook, skip next tr, sl st in next tr; rep from * around—18 picots.

Fasten off.

bluebell

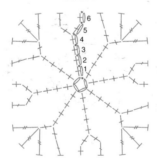

belle flores

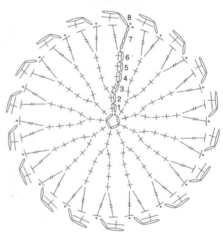

belle flores

bluebell

liliputs

materials

1 .35oz/10g ball (each approx 30yd/27m) of Presencia *Finca No 3* (cotton) in #1214 yellow (B), #1729 pink (A), #7720 peach (A), #1474 salmon (A), #3305 blue (A), #2606 orchid (A) or #8785 grey (A)

Size 00 (3mm) crochet hook

7mm round beads

Note A can be used interchangeably.

With B, ch 5. Join with sl st in first ch to form a ring.

Rnd 1 Ch 1, [1 sc, 2 dc] 5 times in ring. Join with sl st to first sc—15 sts.

Fasten off B and join A.

Rnd 2 Ch 1, *1 sc in next sc, [2 dc, 1 tr] in next dc, [1 tr, 2 dc] in next dc; rep from * 4 times more.
Join with sl st to first sc—35 sts.

Rnd 3 Ch 1, *1 sc in next sc, 2 dc in next st, [1 dc, 1 sc] in next st, [1 sc, 1 dc] in next st, sl st in next st; rep from *, end last rep sl st in first sc.

Fasten off.

Sew bead to center and cup flower in palm to shape.

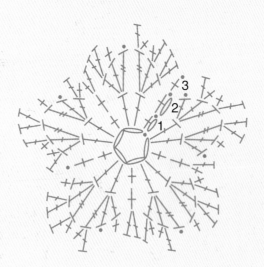

wedding boutonniere

materials

1 2oz/57g ball (approx 191yd/175m) of Coats & Clark *Opera 5 Crochet Thread* (mercerized cotton) in #0500 white

Size C/2 (2.75mm) crochet hook

9mm round beads

Ch 5. Join with sl st in first ch to form a ring.

Rnd 1 Ch 1, 5 sc in ring. Join with sl st to first sc.

Rnd 2 Ch 1, 2 sc in each sc around—10 sc. Join with sl st to first sc.

Rnd 3 Ch 1, 2 sc in each sc around—20 sc. Join with sl st to first sc.

Rnd 4 Working in front lps only, *ch 3, 1 tr in same sc, 2 tr in next 2 sc, 1 tr in next sc, ch 3, sl st in same sc and in next sc; rep from * 4 times more, end last rep sl st in same sc—5 petals.

Rnd 5 Working behind petals, sl st to center of first petal. *Ch 4, 1 dtr in same st, 2 dtr in each of next 2 sts, 1 dtr in next st, ch 4, sl st in same st and in next st; rep from * 4 times more, end last rep sl st in same st—2nd row of 5 petals.

Fasten off.

Sew bead to center of flower.

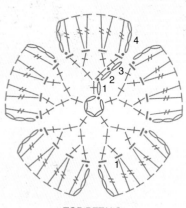

TOP PETALS
RNDS 1–4

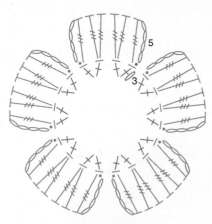

BOTTOM PETALS
RND 5

floral belted shawl

one size

Stole: approx 18"W x 72"L/45.5cm x 183cm

Belt: approx 3½"W x 80"L/9cm x 203cm

gauge

23 st + 10¾ rws=4"/10cm in mesh pattern using larger crochet hook

materials

3 1¾oz/50g skeins (each approx 255yd/230m) of Artyarns *Cashmere 2* (2 stranded cashmere) in #130 (A)

1 1¾oz/50g skein (approx 100yd/90m) of Artyarns *Beaded Silk* (silk/glass beads) in #130 (B)

Sizes H/8 and G/6 (5 and 4mm) crochet hooks

Shawl

With A and larger hook, ch 105.

Row 1 1 sc in 9th ch from hook, *ch 5, skip 3 ch, 1 sc in next ch; rep from * to end—25 ch-lps.

Turn.

Row 2 *Ch 5, 1 sc in next ch-5 sp; rep from * to last ch-sp, ch 5, skip (1sc, 2ch), 1 sc in next ch. Turn.

Row 3 *Ch 5, 1 sc in next ch-5 sp; rep from * to last ch-sp, ch 5, 1 sc in 3rd ch of beg ch. Turn.

Rows 4–53 Rep row 3.

Row 54 Ch 3 (counts as 1 dc), 3 dc in next ch-5 sp, *4 dc in next ch-5 sp; rep from * to last ch-sp, 3 dc in last ch-sp, 1 dc in 3rd ch of beg ch—100 dc. Turn.

Row 55 Ch 3, 1 dc in next dc and in each dc across. Turn.

Row 56 *Ch 5, skip next 3 dc, 1 sc in next dc; rep from *, end last rep 1 sc in 3rd ch of beg ch. Turn.

Row 57 *Ch 5, 1 sc in next ch-5 sp; rep from * to last ch-sp, ch 5, 1 sc in 3rd ch of beg ch. Turn.

Rows 58–67 Rep row 31.

Rows 68–151 Rep rows 54–67 six times more.

Rows 152–190 Rep row 31.

Row 191 Ch 5, *1 sc in next ch-5 sp, ch 3; rep from *, end last rep ch 5, 1 sc in 3rd ch of beg ch. Turn.

floral belted shawl

cont. from previous page

Edging

*Ch 1, 4 sc in each ch-sp across. Working along side edge of shawl, 4 sc in each ch-sp and dc-sp across. Rep from * for rem 2 edges. Join with sl st to first sc.

Belt

With larger hook and B, ch 15.

Row 1 1 sc in 2nd ch from hook and in each rem ch—14 sc. Turn.

Row 2 Ch 3, working through back lps only, 1 dc in each sc across. Turn.

Row 3 Ch 3, 1 dc in each dc across. Turn.

Row 4 Ch 3, working through back lps only, 1 dc in each dc across. Turn.

Rep rows 3 and 4 to desired length.

Last row Sl st in each dc across.

Fasten off.

Ties

With RS facing, join A to foundation ch.

Row 1 Ch 1, 1 sc in each ch across—14 sc. Turn.

Row 2 Ch 5, skip 2 sc, 1 sc in next sc, [ch 5, skip 3 sc, 1 sc in next sc] twice, ch 5, skip 2 sc, 1 sc in last sc—4 ch-5 lps. Turn.

Row 3 *Ch 5, sc in next ch-5 lp; rep from * to end. Turn.

Rows 4–27 Rep row 3.

Fasten off.

Repeat along last row at other end of belt.

Edging

With RS facing, join A to tie where it joins to belt. Ch 1, 4 sc in each ch-sp along 3 edges of tie. Fasten off, using tails to join to edging of belt.

Repeat at other end of tie.

Flowers

Make 15 Wedding Boutonnieres (see page 58) using smaller hook and MC.

Bi-color flowers (make 10)

Add B edgings to 10 flowers as foll:

Inner petals Join CC in first sl st between any 2 petals.

With smaller hook, *sl st in 2 sl st, 2 sc in ch-3 sp, 1 sc in next 6 tr, 2 sc in ch-3 sp; rep from * 3 times more. Join with sl st in first sl st. Fasten off.

Outer petals Join B in first sl st between any 2 petals.

With smaller hook, *sl st in 2 sl st, 3 sc in ch-4 sp, 1 sc in next 6 dtr, 3 sc in ch-4 sp; rep from * 3 times more. Join with sl st in first sl st. Fasten off.

Button center

With smaller hook and B, ch 5, leaving a 6"/15cm tail. Join with sl st in first ch to form a ring.

Rnd 1 Ch 1, 5 sc in ring. Join with sl st to first sc.

Rnds 2 and 3 Ch 1, 1 sc in each sc around. Join with sl st to first sc.

Fasten off.

Cut yarn, leaving a 6"/15cm tail. Thread beg tail through center, tie the 2 tails together to form a button and sew to center of flower.

Finishing

Center belt at bottom edge of stole. Tack in 3 places to secure—at center dc-row and the 2 adjacent dc-rows to either side. Sew a bi-color flower to center of belt.

Sew remaining flowers as desired along top edge of stole, between center 5 dc rows.

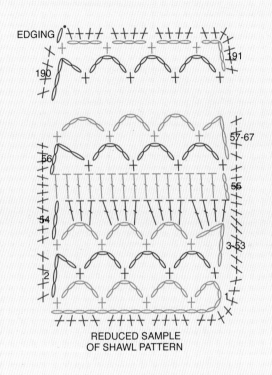

EDGING

191
190

57-67
56
55
54
3-53
2
1

REDUCED SAMPLE
OF SHAWL PATTERN

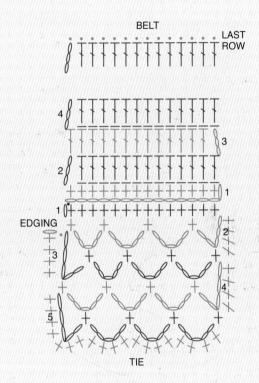

BELT

LAST
ROW

4
2
1

EDGING
3
5

2
4

TIE

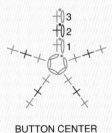

3
2
1

BUTTON CENTER

floral necklette

size

Approx 5½"W x 30"L/14cm x 76.2cm

gauge

8 st x 3½ rws = 2"/5cm in dc st using larger crochet hook

materials

1 3½oz/100g skein (approx 130yd/119m) of Tilli Tomas *Flurries* (wool/glass beads) in moss (A)

1 3½oz/100g skein (approx 120yd/110m) of Tilli Tomas *Ritz* (silk with madeira/glass beads) in multi blue-green (B)

1 3½oz/100g skein (approx 120yd/110m) of Tilli Tomas *Asteroid* (silk/glass beads) in moroccan blue (C)

Size I/9 and J/10 (5.5 and 6mm) crochet hooks

Base

With larger hook and B, ch 10.

Row 1 1 dc in 7th ch from hook and in each ch to end—4-dc. Turn.

Row 2 Ch 6, 1 dc in each dc to end—4 dc. Turn.

Rows 3–24 Rep row 2.

Row 25 Ch 6, 1 dc in first 2 dc, 1 hdc in next dc, 1 sc in last dc. Turn.

Row 26 Ch 6, 1 sc in sc, 1 hdc in hdc, 1 dc in next 2 dc. Turn.

Rows 27–30 Rep rows 25 and 26.

Row 31 Ch 6, 1 dc in first 2 dc, 1 hdc in hdc, 1 sc in sc. Turn.

Row 32 Ch 3, insert hook through 3 inner ch-6 lps, yo and draw through lp on hook, ch 3, 1 sc in sc, 1 hdc in hdc, 1 dc in next 2 dc. Turn.

Row 33 Ch 6, 1 dc in each st to end—4 dc. Turn.

Row 34 Ch 3, insert hook through next inner ch-6 lp, yo and draw through lp on hook, ch 3, 1 dc in each st—4 dc. Turn.

Row 35 Ch 6, 1 dc in each dc—4 dc. Turn.

Rows 36–55 Rep rows 34 and 35.

Row 56 Rep row 34.

Rows 57–64 Rep rows 25 through 32.

floral necklette

cont. from previous page

Using sl st, join first and last rows.

Fasten off.

Embellishment

Flowers With smaller hook, make 16 Narcisse (see page 48) as foll: 4 A, 8 B, 4 C. Place randomly along solid areas of base.

Button With smaller hook and MC, make 1 Bloomin' Ball (see page 122) and sew in place 3"/7.5cm from one end of base. Slip button through any loop to keep necklet in place.

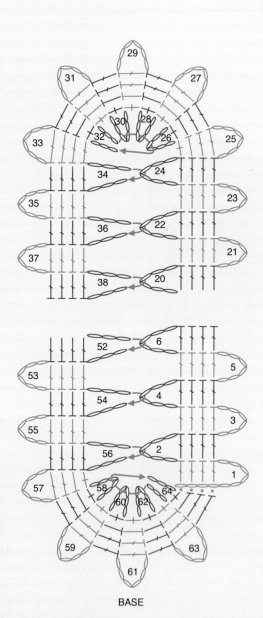

BASE

**BLOOMIN' BALL
RNDS 1–3**

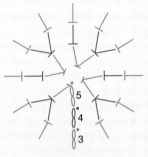

**BLOOMIN' BALL
RNDS 3–5**

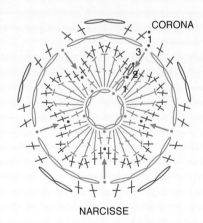

CORONA

NARCISSE

chapter three

twisted-technique flowers

Unlike many of the flowers in Chapters 1 and 2, these flowers are made in easy pattern stitches and then twisted and sewn into shape. The pattern stitches are classic crochet edgings such as scallops, corkscrews, loop stitches, ruffles and fringes.

The size of the flowers can be easily adjusted by crocheting shorter or longer pieces before twisting. The weight of the yarn is also a major factor in the size of your flowers. Traditional crocheted flowers were made in #3, #5 or #10 cotton thread, but in this book I have mainly focused on using heavier yarn weights to update the look and use of crocheted flowers.

corkscrews

cascade corkscrew • corkscrew daisy • corkscrew blossom • crowning corkscrew • spoke corkscrew flower • corkscrew pansy

materials

1 1¾oz/50g skein (approx 175yd/160m) of Koigu Wool Designs *KPPPM* (wool) in #P129 (A)

1 1¾oz/50g skein (approx 170yd/153m) of Koigu Wool Designs *KPM* (wool) in #2343 (B)

1 1¾oz/50g skein (each approx 114yd/104m) of Koigu Wool Designs *Kersti Merino Crepe* (wool) in #2232 (C) and #605 (D)

Size C/2 (2.75mm) crochet hook

Cascade Corkscrew

(Make 4)

With A, ch 25.

Row 1 3 sc in 2nd ch from hook and in each ch to end—72 sc.

Fasten off.

Overlap corkscrews at center point and sew in place.

Corkscrew Daisy

Center

With B, ch 4. Join with sl st in first ch to form a ring.

Rnd 1 Ch 3 (counts as 1 dc), 9 dc in ring—10 dc. Join with sl st in top of ch.

Rnd 2 Ch 1, 1 sc in each dc around—10 sc. Join with sl st to first sc.

Fasten off.

Petals

(make 5)

With A, ch 25.

Row 1 3 sc in 2nd ch from hook and in each ch to end—72 sc.

Fasten off.

Twist petal so it corkscrews and tie beg and end tails to secure. Using tails, attach to center at every other sc.

cascade corkscrew

REDUCED SAMPLE OF PATTERN

corkscrew daisy

REDUCED SAMPLE OF
PETAL PATTERN

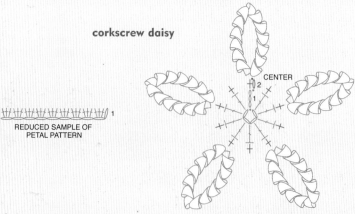

CENTER

CONTRUCTON DIAGRAM

corkscrew blossom

corkscrew pansy

cascade
corkscrew

spoke corkscrew

crowning corkscrew

corkscrew
daisy

corkscrews

cont. from previous page

Corkscrew Blossom

Center

With C, ch 4. Join with sl st in first ch to form a ring.

Rnd 1 Ch 4 (counts as 1 tr), 16 tr in ring—17 tr. Join with sl st in top of ch.

Rnd 2 Ch 1, 2 sc in each sc around—34 sc. Join with sl st to first sc.

Fasten off.

Petals (make 1)

With B, ch 35.

Row 1 2 tr in 4th ch from hook, 3 tr in each ch to end.

Fasten off, leaving a long tail.

Twist corkscrew and sew in place using tail around edge of center.

Crowning Corkscrew

Outer petal

With B, work 3 rnds of Small Snowball (see page 82).

Inner petal

With B, ch 20.

Row 1 2 tr in 4th ch from hook, 3 tr in each ch to end.

Fasten off, leaving a long tail.

Twist corkscrew and sew in place using tail at center of outer petal.

crowning corkscrew

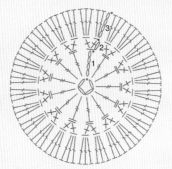

OUTER PETALS

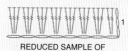

REDUCED SAMPLE OF
INNER PETALS PATTERN

INNER PETALS

corkscrew blossom

CENTER WITH PETALS

REDUCED SAMPLE OF
PETAL PATTERN

Spoke Corkscrew Flower

Spokes

With A, ch 12. Join with sl st in first ch to form a ring.

Rnd 1 *Ch 7, 1 sc in 2nd ch from hook, 1 sl st in next 5 ch, 1 sc in next ch of ring; rep from * around—12 spokes.

Fasten off.

Center

With A, ch 25.

Row 1 2 tr in 4th ch from hook, 3 tr in each ch to end.

Fasten off, leaving a long tail.

Twist corkscrew and center on top of spokes. Sew in place using tail.

Corkscrew Pansy

With D, ch 20.

Row 1 2 tr in 4th ch from hook, 3 tr in each ch to end.

Fasten off.

Twist to form petals and sew beg to end using tails.

spoke corkscrew flower

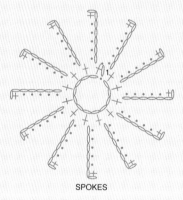

SPOKES

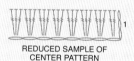

REDUCED SAMPLE OF
CENTER PATTERN

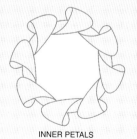

INNER PETALS

corkscrew pansy

REDUCED SAMPLE OF
PATTERN

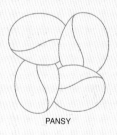

PANSY

blue rose trio

secondhand rose • ruffle rose • rosette

materials

1 1¾oz/50g skein (each approx 138yd/124m) of Alchemy Yarns of Transformation *Silk Purse* (silk) in #02w deep sea (A) and #82w janboy's sapphire (B)

Size C/2 (2.75mm) crochet hook

Secondhand Rose

With A, Ch 54.

Row 1 1 dc in 4th ch from hook and in each ch to end. Ch 3, turn.

Row 2 [1 dc, ch 2, 2 dc] in first dc, *skip 2 dc, [2 dc, ch 2, 2 dc] in next dc; rep from * to end. Ch 3, turn.

Row 3 6 dc in first ch-2 sp, 1 sc in next ch-2 sp, *7 dc in next ch-2 sp, 1 sc in next ch-2 sp; rep from *, end last rep with sl st in last ch-2 sp.

Fasten off.

For two-tone roses, work tops of petals with a different color as foll:

Row 4 ch1, sc in sl st, sc in each dc and sc across. Fasten off.

Roll into a spiral and sew in place.

Ruffle Rose

With B, ch 40.

Row 1 With B, 4 tr in 4th ch from hook, [with B, 5 tr in next ch] 7 times, [with A, 5 tr in next ch] 7 times, [with B, 5 tr in next ch] 9 times, [with A, 5 tr in next ch] 13 times.

Fasten off.

Roll into a spiral and sew in place.

Rosette

With A, Ch 16.

Row 1 4 tr in 4th ch from hook, 5 tr in each ch to end.

Fasten off.

Roll into a spiral and sew in place.

For larger rosettes, make a longer chain or use a heavier yarn and larger hook.

ruffle rose

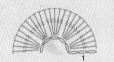

REDUCED SAMPLE OF PATTERN

rosette

REDUCED SAMPLE OF PATTERN

secondhand rose

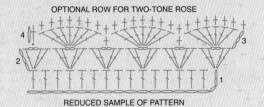

REDUCED SAMPLE OF PATTERN

ruffle rose

rosette

secondhand rose

roseys

materials

1 1¾oz/50g skein (each approx 61yd/55m) of Muench Yarns *Touch Me* (rayon microfiber/wool) in #3647 magenta (A), #3642 rose (B), #3608 hot pink (C) and #3636 lt green (D)

Size G/6 (4mm) crochet hook

Size F/5 (3.75mm) crochet hook for leaf

Petals

With larger hook and A, B or C, ch 54.

Row 1 (RS) 2 sc in 2nd ch from hook, *skip next ch, 5 dc in next ch, skip next ch, 2 sc in next ch; rep from * to end—13 shells.

Row 2 Working on other side of foundation ch, 1 sc in each ch to end.

Fasten off.

Roll into a spiral so petals lie flat and sew in place.

Leaf

With smaller hook and D, ch 5.

Stem row 1 sc in 2nd ch from hook and in each ch to end—4 sc.

Row 1 Ch 1, working into side of last sc, 3 sc in end st. Ch 1, turn.

Row 2 2 sc in first sc, 1 sc in next sc, 2 sc in last sc—5 sc. Ch 1, turn.

Rows 3, 5, 7 and 9 1 sc in each sc to end. Ch 1, turn.

Row 4 1 sc in first sc, 2 sc in next sc, 1 sc in next sc, 2 sc in next sc, 1 sc in last sc—7 sc. Ch 1, turn.

Row 6 1 sc in first sc, [sc2tog, 1 sc in next sc] twice—5 sc. Ch 1, turn.

Row 8 Sc2tog, 1 sc in next sc, sc2tog—3 sts. Ch 1, turn.

Row 10 Sc3tog.

Fasten off.

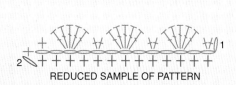

REDUCED SAMPLE OF PATTERN

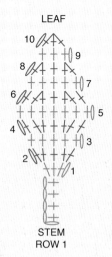

LEAF

STEM
ROW 1

spider and loopy

materials (spider flower)

1 1¾oz/50g ball (approx 82yd/75m) of Lion Brand Yarn *Moonlight Mohair* (acrylic/mohair/cotton/metallic polyester) in #210 painted desert

Size F/5 (3.75mm) crochet hook

materials (loopy flower)

1 1¾oz/50g skein (approx 82yd/75m) of Lion Brand Yarn *Moonlight Mohair* (acrylic/mohair/cotton/metallic polyester) in #207 coral reef

Size F/5 (3.75mm) crochet hook

Spider Flower

Row 1 *Ch 8, 1 sl st in 2nd ch from hook and in each ch to end; rep from * 47 times more.

Fasten off, leaving a long tail.

Roll in a spiral to form flower, using tail to sew in place as you roll.

Loopy Flower

Crochet a chain 8"/20cm in length.

Row 1 1 sc in 2nd ch from hook and in each ch to end. Turn.

Row 2 (loops) Ch 1, insert hook in next sc, wind yarn twice around 2 fingers of LH, bring working yarn from behind fingers, insert hook under all strands and pull up a lp, yo and draw through all lps; rep from * to end.

Fasten off, leaving a long tail.

Roll in a spiral to form flower, using tail to sew in place as you roll.

spider flower

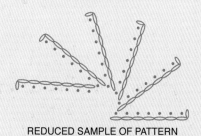

REDUCED SAMPLE OF PATTERN

loopy flower

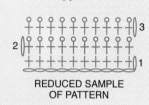

REDUCED SAMPLE
OF PATTERN

loopy flower

spider flower

snowballs

large snowball • small snowball • fan flower

materials

1 1¾oz/50g skein (each approx 83yd/75m) of S. Charles/Takhi•Stacy Charles, Inc. Merino Cable (wool) in #137 rose (A), #lilac (B) or #102 beige (C)

Size F/5 (3.75mm) crochet hook

Note In photo, small flower is resting on fan flower.

Large Snowball

With A, ch 4. Join with sl st in first ch to form a ring.

Rnd 1 Ch 2 (counts as 1 hdc), 7 hdc in ring. Join with sl st to first hdc.

Rnd 2 Ch 2 (counts as 1 hdc), hdc in same sp, 2 hdc in each hdc around—16 hdc. Join with sl st to first hdc.

Rnds 3 and 4 Working in back lps only, ch 1, 1 sc in each st around. Join with sl st to first sc.

Rnd 5 Working in back lps only, ch 1, 3 sc in each sc around—48 sc. Join with sl st to first sc.

Rnd 6 Working in back lps only, ch 3 (counts as 1 dc), 2 dc in same sp, 3 dc in each sc around—144 dc. Join with sl st in top of beg ch. Turn.

Rnd 7 *Ch 5, sc in next dc; rep from * around. Join with sl st in first ch of beg ch.

Fasten off.

large snowball

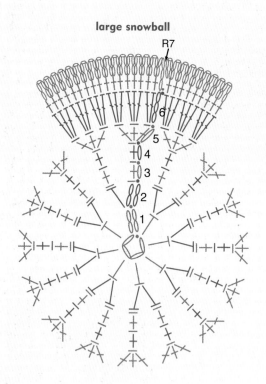

snowballs

cont. from previous page

Small Snowball

With B, ch 4. Join with sl st in first ch to form a ring.

Rnd 1 Ch 4 (counts as 1 tr), 12 tr in ring. Join with sl st in top of beg ch.

Rnd 2 Working in back lps only, ch 1, 2 sc in each sc around—26 sc. Join with sl st to first sc.

Rnd 3 Working in back lps only, ch 3, 2 dc in same sp, 3 dc in each sc around—

78 dc. Join with sl st in top of beg ch. Turn.

Rnd 4 *Ch 5, sc in next dc; rep from * around. Join with sl st in first ch of beg ch.

Fasten off.

Fan Flower

With C, ch 4. Join with sl st in first ch to form a ring.

Rnd 1 Ch 3 (counts as 1 dc), 12 dc in ring. Join with sl st in top of beg ch.

Rnd 2 Working in back lps only, ch 4, 2 tr in same sp, 3 tr in each dc around—39 tr. Join with sl st in top of beg ch. Turn.

Rnd 3 *Ch 5, sc in next tr; rep from * around. Join with sl st in first ch of beg ch.

Fasten off.

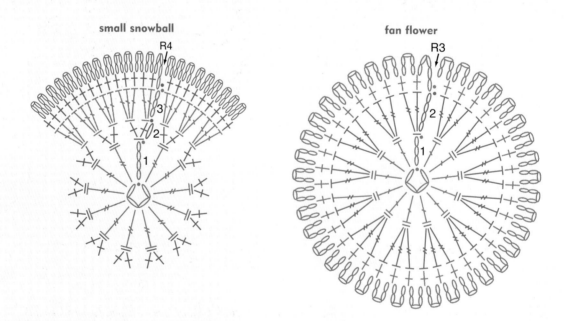

small snowball

fan flower

st. margaret's flower

star-spangled bead

star-spangled bead *and* st. margaret's flower

materials (star-spangled bead)

1 1¾oz/50g skein (each approx 100yd/90m) of Artyarns *Beaded Silk* (silk/glass beads) in #149 or #144

Size G/6 (4mm) crochet hook

materials (st. margaret's flower)

1 3½oz/100g skein (each approx 120yd/110m) of Tilli Tomas *Ritz* (silk with madeira/glass beads) in ethereal delight

1 3½oz/100g skein (each approx 130yd/119m) of Tilli Tomas *Flurries* (wool/glass beads) in dusty purple

Size G/6 (4mm) crochet hook

star-spangled bead and *st. margaret's flower*

cont. from previous page

Star-Spangled Bead

Ch 4. Join with sl st in first ch to form
a ring.

Rnd 1 Ch 1, 10 sc in ring. Join with sl st
to first sc. Turn.

Rnd 2 *Ch 2, 5 sc in 2nd ch from hook, sl
st in front lp of next sc; rep from *, end sl
st in base of beg ch-2 to join—10 petals.

Rnd 3 Working behind row 2, *ch 7, 1 sc
in 2nd ch from hook, 1 hdc in next ch, 4
dc in next 4 ch, 1 sc in back lp of next 2
sc of rnd 2; rep from * around—5 petals.
Join with sl st in base of beg ch-7.

Fasten off.

star-spangled bead

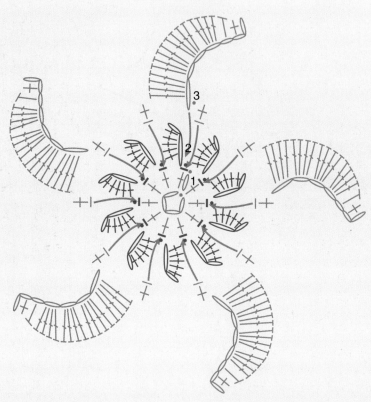

St. Margaret's Flower

5/10-st Bullion Wrap yarn loosely around hook the number of times specified, pick up a lp in next st, yo and draw through all lps on hook, pulling up to height of wraps, ch 1.

Ch 4. Join with sl st in first ch to form a ring.

Rnd 1 Ch 1, 10 sc in ring. Join with sl st to first sc.

Rnd 2 *Ch 2, 3 dc in next sc, ch 2, sl st in next st; rep from * 4 times more—5 petals.

Rnd 3 (loops) Working behind row 2, *ch 3, 1 sc in bottom center of next petal; rep from * 4 times more—5 ch-3 lps.

Rnd 4 (bullions) Sl st in first ch-3 lp, *ch 2, [5-wrap bullion, 10-wrap bullion, 5-wrap bullion] in same ch-3 lp, ch 3, sl st in same lp, 1 sc in next ch-3 lp; rep from * 4 times more—5 petals. Join with sl st to first sl st.

Rnd 5 Working behind row 4, *ch 12, sl st in same st, ch 5, skip bullion petal, sl st between next 2 petals; rep from * 4 times more—5 ch-12 petals. Join with sl st in joining sl st.

Fasten off.

st. margaret's flower

carnival and metal mix

materials

1 1¾oz/50g skein (each approx 115yd/105m) of Lion Brand Yarn *Glitterspun* (acrylic/cupro/polyester) in #135 bronze (A), #170 gold (B), #150 silver (C) and #153 onyx (D)

Size F/5 (3.75mm) crochet hook

Size H/8 (5mm) crochet hook

One decorative button

Carnival

Center

With larger hook and B, ch 4. Join with sl st in first ch to form a ring.

Rnd 1 Ch 1, 12 sc in ring. Join with sl st to first sc. Fasten off B.

Rnd 2 Join A, ch 2 (counts as 1 hdc), [1 hdc, ch 2, 1 hdc] in next sc, *hdc in next sc, [hdc, ch 2, hdc] in next sc; rep from * 4 times more—6 ch-2 sp. Join with sl st in top of beg ch. Fasten off A.

Rnd 3 Join C, ch 2 (counts as 1 hdc), 1 hdc in next hdc, *[1 hdc, ch 2, 1 hdc] in next ch-2 sp, 1 hdc in next 3 hdc; rep from *, end last rep 1 hdc in last hdc. Join with sl st in top of beg ch. Fasten off C.

Rnd 4 Join D, ch 2 (counts as 1 hdc), 1 hdc in next 2 hdc, *ch 2, 1 hdc in next 5 hdc; rep from *, end last rep 1 hdc in last 2 hdc. Join with sl st in top of beg ch. Fasten off D.

Popcorn (pop) rnd

Join A to ch-2 sp. Ch 3, 7 dc in ch-2 sp. Sl lp from hook, insert hook in top of beg ch, place lp back on hook and draw through beg ch. Ch 1 to secure. Fasten off.

Rep pop for each ch-2 sp, alternating colors—6 pops.

Petal twist

With A, ch 6.

Row 1 1 dc in 4th ch from hook and in each ch to end—4 sts. Turn.

Rows 2 Ch 3, 1 dc in each ch to end. Turn.

Rep row 2 until there are 6 rows A. Fasten off.

Cont to work 6 rows of each rem color—24 rows.

Twist to form petals and sew to rnd 3 of center.

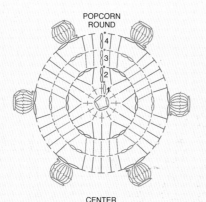

POPCORN ROUND

CENTER

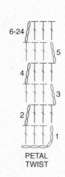

carnival

PETAL TWIST

PETAL TWIST

carnival

metal mix

carnival and metal mix

cont. from previous page

Metal Mix

Center

With smaller hook and B, ch 4. Join with sl st in first ch to form a ring.

Rnd 1 Ch 1, 12 sc in ring. Join with sl st to first sc. Fasten off B.

Rnd 2 Join A, ch 2 (counts as 1 hdc), [1 hdc, ch 2, 1 hdc] in next sc, *hdc in next sc, [hdc, ch 2, hdc] in next sc; rep from * 4 times more—6 corners. Join with sl st in top of beg ch. Fasten off A.

Rnd 3 Join C, ch 2 (counts as 1 hdc), 1 hdc in next hdc, *ch 2, 1 hdc in next 3 hdc; rep from *, end last rep 1 hdc in last hdc. Join with sl st in top of beg ch. Fasten off C.

Rnd 4 Join D, rep rnd 3.

Fasten off D.

Coils

Join A to ch-2 sp.

Row 1 Ch 3, 1 dc in next 3 hdc—4 dc. Turn.

Rows 2–7 Ch 3, 1 dc in next 3 dc. Turn.

Row 8 Ch 1, 1 dc in next 4 dc.

Fasten off.

Rep rows 1–8 for each side of center, alternating colors—6 coils.

Fold each coil behind an adjacent coil and sew in place. Sew button to center.

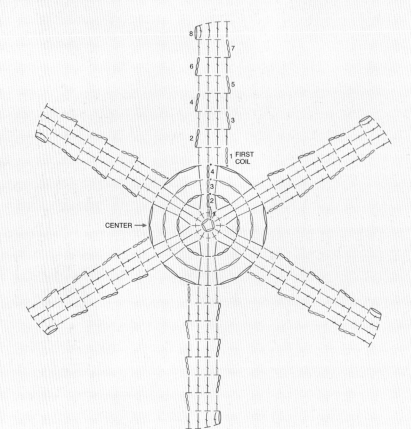

metal mix

8
7
6
5
4
3
2
1 FIRST COIL

4
3
2
1

CENTER →

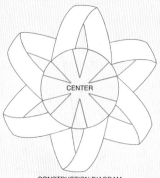

CENTER

CONSTRUCTION DIAGRAM

calla lily bridal bouquet

materials

1 1¾oz/50g spool (each approx 145yd/130m) of Fonty/Russi Sales *Serpentine* in #830 milk (A), #927 apricot (B), #826 goldenrod (C) and #919 forest (D)

Size D/3 (3.25mm) crochet hook

2yd/2m of 3"/7.6cm-wide ribbon

16" Flora wire (pkg of 8)

½" white Flora tape

Sprigs of artificial leaves or filler

Spathe (make 9: 5 with A and 4 with B)

Ch 4.

Rnd 1 11 dc in 4th ch from hook— 12 dc. Join with sl st in first ch.

Rnd 2 Ch 3 (counts as 1 dc throughout), 1 dc in same st, 2 dc in each dc around—24 dc. Join with sl st in top of beg ch.

Rnd 3 Ch 3, 1 dc in same st, 2 dc in next 7 dc, [ch 1, 1 dc in next dc] 9 times, ch 1, 2 dc in next 7 dc—39 dc, 10 ch-1 sp. Join with sl st in top of beg ch.

Rnd 4 Ch 3, 1 dc in same st, [1 dc in next dc, 2 dc in next dc] 7 times, [ch 2, dc in next ch-sp] 10 times, ch 2, skip next dc, [1 dc in next dc, 2 dc in next dc] 6 times, 1 dc in last dc—52 dc, 11 ch-2 sp. Join with sl st.

Rnd 5 Ch 3, 1 dc in same sp, [1 dc in next 2 dc, 2 dc in next dc] 7 times, [1 dc in

next dc, 3 dc in next ch-2 sp] 5 times, 1 tr in next dc, [1 tr, 1 dtr] in next ch-2 sp, ch 2, sl st in top of previous dtr, [1 dtr, 1 tr] in same sp, 1 tr in next dc, [3 dc in next ch-sp, 1 dc in next dc] 5 times, [2 dc in next dc, 1 dc in next 2 dc] 6 times. Join with sl st in top of beg ch.

Fasten off.

Base

With D, ch 2.

Rnd 1 6 sc in first ch. Join with sl st to first sc.

Rnd 2 Ch 1, 2 sc in each sc around—12 sc. Join with sl st to first sc.

Rnd 3 Ch 1, *1 sc in next 3 sc, 2 sc in next sc; rep from * around—15 sc. Join with sl st to first sc.

Rnds 4–12 Ch 1, 1 sc in each sc around. Join with sl st to first sc. Fasten off.

calla lily bridal bouquet

cont. from previous page

Spadix

With C, ch 21.

Row 1 1 sc in 2nd ch from hook and in each ch to end.

Fasten off.

Finishing

Sew base of spadix to end of rnd of spathe. Roll spathe to enclose spadix, tack closed and insert into base. Cut a length of flora wire, place on stem and sew seam of stem to enclose. Sew end of stem to base of flower. Arrange flowers and filler as desired and tape wires with flora tape. Wind ribbon around stems to enclose and tie a bow at top of stems.

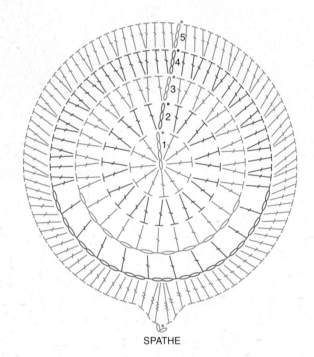

SPATHE

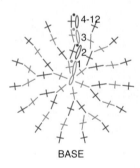

BASE

SPADIX

ecru roses for wedding dress

materials

4 3½oz/100g skeins (each approx 120yd/110m) of Tilli Tomas *Mariel's Crystals* (silk/crystal beads) in natural

Size G/6 (4mm) crochet hook

Sewing needle and matching thread

Gown purchased from J. Crew bridal collection

Large Rose (make 18)

Follow instructions for Secondhand Rose (see page 74).

Small Rose (make 20)

Ch 35.

Row 1 1 sc in 2nd ch from hook and in each chain across—34 sc. Turn.

Row 2 Ch 3, [1 dc, ch 2, 2 dc] in first sc, *skip 2 sc, [2 dc, ch 2, 2 dc] in next sc; rep from * to end. Turn.

Row 3 Ch 3, 6 dc in first ch-2 sp, 1 sc in next ch-2 sp, *7 dc in next ch-2 sp, 1 sc in next ch-2 sp; rep from *, end last rep sl st in last ch-2 sp.

Fasten off.

Finishing

Roll into a spiral and sew in place.

Position flowers as desired and sew in place using sewing needle and thread.

large rose

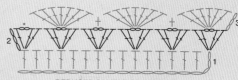

REDUCED SAMPLE OF PATTERN

small rose

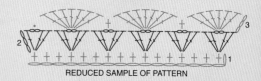

REDUCED SAMPLE OF PATTERN

chapter four felted flowers

I'm often asked if crocheted flowers can be felted like knitted flowers. The answer is yes! However, you have to make them out of natural-fiber yarn like pure wool or alpaca, or yarn containing at least 50% animal fibers.

The striped folk daisy and the rose are cut flowers. (The cut rose was so popular in my Knitted Flowers *book that I decided to include a crocheted version in this book.) To make it, form a rectangle out of single crochet. Then felt this piece, use the templates to cut out the petals and sew them together.*

The other flowers in this chapter are crocheted to the desired shape (rather than cut) before felting. They are also pretty without felting. If you have never felted before, small projects like flowers are a nice way to begin.

Note that the black and blue flower pin has vintage buttons in the center. You may have a few of these lying around that will look great, or you can use new buttons.

striped folk daisy

materials

1 3oz/85g ball (each approx 158yd/144m) of Lion Brand Yarn *Lion Wool* (wool) in #153 ebony (A) and #132 lemongrass (B)

Size H/8 (5mm) crochet hook

Embroidery floss and needle

With A, ch 40.

Row 1 1 Sc in 2nd ch from hook and in each ch across —39 sc. Turn.

Row 2 Ch 1, 1 sc in each sc across.

Rep row 2, changing colors every 4 rows for 40 rows total.

Fasten off.

Finishing

Felt fabric (see page 144) until individual stitches are no longer visible.

Using templates, cut 5 petals of each size and 1 circle from felt. Sew 5 larger petals together at center. Sew 5 smaller petals together at center. Center small flower on large flower, center circle on small flower and sew 3 layers together. Embellish circle with whipstitch and French knot if desired.

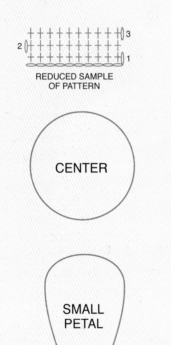

REDUCED SAMPLE OF PATTERN

CENTER

SMALL PETAL

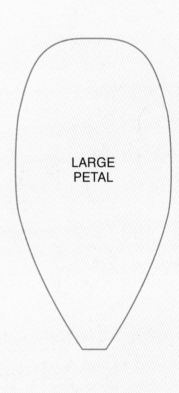

LARGE PETAL

cut rose

materials

1 1¾oz/50g skein (approx 55yd/49m) of Nashua Handknits/Westminster Fibers, Inc. *Painted Forest* in #200 jewels

Size H/8 (5mm) hook

Ch 45.

Row 1 1 sc in 2nd ch from hook and in each ch across. Turn.

Row 2 Ch 1, sc in each sc across. Turn.

Rep row 2 until skein is finished.

Fasten off.

Finishing

Felt fabric (see page 144). Press flat before drying. When completely dry, use templates to cut out 5 petals, 1 center and 3 leaves for each rose. Form spiral with center, beg with short side in and sew in place. Sew 5 petals evenly around base of center, overlapping as needed. Place leaves as desired and sew in place.

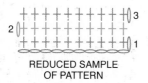

REDUCED SAMPLE
OF PATTERN

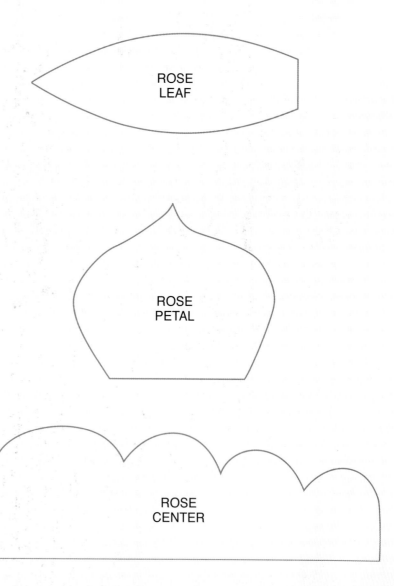

ROSE
LEAF

ROSE
PETAL

ROSE
CENTER

vintage roses

materials

1 3oz/85g skein (each approx 158yd/144m) of Lion Brand Yarn *Lion Wool* (wool) in #140 rose (A) and #113 scarlet (B)

Size J/10 (6mm) crochet hook

Rose

With A, ch 11 (20, 33)"/28 (51, 81.5)cm.

Row 1 2 sc in 2nd ch from hook and in each ch to end. Turn.

Row 2 Ch 2 (counts as 1 hdc), 3 hdc in first sc, 4 hdc in each sc to end. Turn.

Row 3 Ch 3, 1 dc in same sp, 2 dc in each hdc to end. Turn.

Fasten off A and join B.

Row 4 Ch 1, 1 sc in each sc to end.

Fasten off, leaving a long tail.

Finishing

Roll strip into a spiral, using tail to sew in place. Felt roses (see page 144), pulling into shape as necessary.

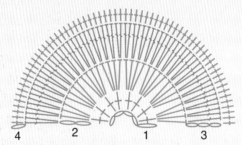

REDUCED SAMPLE OF PATTERN

calla lilies

small calla lily • large calla lily

materials

1 ¾oz/50g skein (each approx 89yd/80m) of GGH/Muench Yarns *Savanna* (alpaca/linen/wool/nylon) in #011 white (A), #013 lime (B) and #030 green (C)

Size F/5 (3.75mm) crochet hook

Size H/8 (5mm) crochet hook

Flora wire (optional)

Small Calla Lily

Spathe

With smaller hook and A, ch 4.

Rnd 1 11 Dc in 4th ch from hook—12 dc. Join with sl st in top of beg ch.

Rnd 2 Ch 3, 1 dc in same st, 2 dc in each dc around—24 dc. Join with sl st in top of beg ch.

Rnd 3 Ch 3, 1 dc in same st, 2 dc in next 6 dc, [ch 2, dc in next dc] 10 times, ch 2, 2 dc in next 7 dc. Join with sl st in top of beg ch.

Rnd 4 Ch 3, 1 dc in same st, [1 dc in next 2 sts, 2 dc in next st] 4 times, [1 dc in next dc, 3 dc in next ch-2 sp] 5 times, 1 tr in next dc, [1 tr, 1 dtr, ch 2] in next ch-2 sp, sl st in top of previous dtr, [1 dtr, 1 tr] in same sp, 1 tr in next dc, [3 dc in next ch-2 sp, 1 dc in next dc] 5 times, [2 dc in next dc, 1 dc in next 2 dc] 4 times, 2 dc in last dc. Join with sl st in top of beg ch.

Fasten off.

Spadix

With B, ch 21.

Row 1 1 sc in 2nd ch from hook and in

small calla lilly

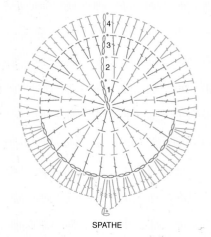

SPATHE

SPADIX

large calla lilly

small calla lilly

each ch to end.

Fasten off.

Base

With C, ch 2.

Rnd 1 6 sc in first ch. Join with sl st to form a ring.

Rnd 2 Ch 1, 2 sc in each sc around—12 sc. Join with sl st to first sc.

Rnd 3 Ch 1, *1 sc in next 3 sc, 2 sc in next sc; rep from * around—15 sc. Join with sl st to first sc.

Rnds 4–10 Ch 1, 1 sc in each sc around. Join with sl st to first sc.

Fasten off.

Stem

With C, chain to desired length.

Row 1 1 sc in 2nd ch from hook and in each ch to end. Turn.

Rows 2 and 3 Ch 1, 1 sc in each sc to end. Turn.

Fasten off.

Finishing

Sew base of spadix to end of rnd of spathe. Roll spathe to enclose spadix, tack closed and insert into base. Cut a length of floral wire, place on stem and sew seam of stem to enclose. Sew end of stem to base of flower and bend stem as desired.

Large Calla Lily

Spathe

With larger hook and B, ch 4.

Rnd 1 11 Dc in 4th ch from hook—12 dc. Join with sl st in top of beg ch.

Rnd 2 Ch 3, 1 dc in same st, 2 dc in each dc around—24 dc. Join with sl st in top of beg ch.

Rnd 3 Ch 3, 1 dc in same st, 2 dc in next 7 dc, [ch 2, dc in next dc] 8 times, ch 2, 2 dc in next 8 dc. Join with sl st in top of beg ch.

Rnd 4 Ch 3, 1 dc in same st, [1 dc in next dc, 2 dc in next dc] 7 times, 1 dc in next dc, [ch 2, 2 dc in ch-2 sp] 9 times, ch 2, [1 dc in next dc, 2 dc in next dc] 8 times. Join with sl st in beg ch.

Rnd 5 Ch 3, 1 dc in same st, [1 dc in next 2 dc, 2 dc in next dc] 7 times, 1 dc in next 2 dc, [3 dc in ch-2 sp, 1 dc in sp between next 2-dc group of rnd 4] 4 times, [1 tr, 1 dtr] in next ch-2 sp, ch 2, sl st in top of previous dtr, [1 dtr, 1 tr] in same sp, [1 dc in sp between next 2-dc group of rnd 4, 3 dc in next ch-2 sp] 5 times, [1 dc in next 2 dc, 2 dc in next dc] 8 times. Join with sl st in top of beg ch.

Fasten off.

Spadix

With larger hook and A, work same as small flower.

Base

With larger hook and C, work same as small flower.

Spathe and stem

With larger hook and C, work same as small flower.

Finishing

Same as small flower. Felt flower (see page 144).

large calla lilly

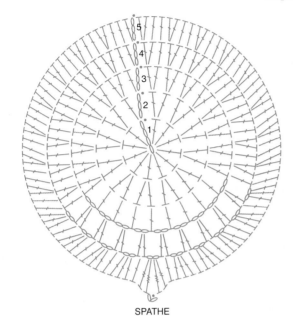

SPATHE

SPADIX

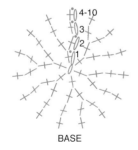

BASE

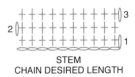

STEM
CHAIN DESIRED LENGTH

passionflower

materials

1 3oz/85g skein (each approx 158yd/144m) of Lion Brand Yarn *Lion Wool* (wool) in #140 rose, #132 lemongrass, #187 goldenrod, #113 scarlet, #147 purple, #178 dk teal and #125 cocoa

Size J/10 (6mm) crochet hook

Petal group (make 2)

*Ch 18.

Row 1 Sl st in 2nd ch from hook, 1 sc in next ch, 1 hdc in next ch, 1 dc in next 4 ch, 1 tr in next 5 ch, 1 dc in next 2 ch, 1 hdc in next ch, 1 sc in next ch, sl st in last ch.

Rep from * 5 times more—6 petals.

Fasten off, leaving a long tail.

Bobble (make 3)

Ch 5. Join with sl st in first ch to form a ring.

Rnd 1 Ch 3 (counts as 1 dc), 17 dc in ring —18 dc. Join with sl st in top of beg ch.

Fasten off, leaving a long tail. Thread tail through edge of bobble, pull tightly to gather and secure.

Finishing

Using tails, sew petal groups into 2 rings of 6 petals each. Center one over the other and sew securely in place. Sew bobbles to center of flower. Felt flower (see page 144), curling petals before allowing flower to dry.

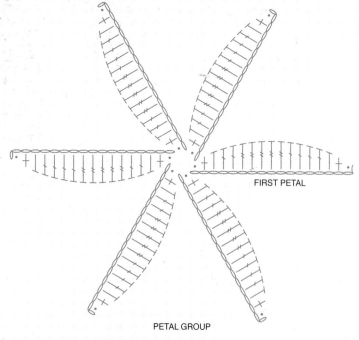

FIRST PETAL

PETAL GROUP

BOBBLE

trumpets

materials

1 1½oz/40g ball (approx 84yd/71m) of Lion Brand Yarn *Lion Cashmere Blend* (wool/nylon/cashmere) in #098 cream, #149 charcoal or #153 black

Size F/5 (3.75mm) crochet hook

Outer flower

Ch 4. Join with sl st in first ch to form a ring.

Rnd 1 Ch 3, 8 dc in ring—9 dc. Join with sl st in top of beg ch.

Rnd 2 Ch 3, 1 dc in each dc around. Join with sl st in top of beg ch.

Rnds 3 and 4 Ch 3, 2 dc in next dc, *1 dc in next 2 dc, 2 dc in next dc; rep from * to last st, 1 dc in last dc—16 dc after rnd 4. Join with sl st in top of beg ch.

Rnd 5 Ch 3, *2 dc in next dc, 1 dc in next dc; rep from * around, end last rep 2 dc in last dc—24 dc. Join with sl st in top of beg ch.

Rnd 6 Ch 3, 1 dc in each dc around. Join with sl st in top of beg ch.

Rnd 7 Ch 3, 1 dc in same st, *3 tr in next st, 2 dc in next st, sl st in next st, 2 dc in next st; rep from * around, ending last rep with sl st in last st—6 petals. Join with sl st in top of beg ch.

Fasten off.

Inner flower

Ch 4. Join with sl st in first ch to form a ring.

Rnd 1 Ch 3, 8 dc in ring—9 dc. Join with sl st in top of beg ch.

Rnd 2 Ch 3, 1 dc in each dc around. Join with sl st in top of beg ch.

Rnds 3 and 4 Ch 3, 2 dc in next dc, *1 dc in next 2 dc, 2 dc in next dc; rep from * to last st, 1 dc in last dc—16 dc after rnd 4. Join with sl st in top of beg ch.

Rnd 5 Ch 3, 1 dc in each dc around. Join with sl st in top of beg ch.

Rnd 6 Ch 3, 1 dc in same st, *3 tr in next st, 2 dc in next st, sl st in next st, 2 dc in next st; rep from * around, end last rep with sl st in last st—4 petals. Join with sl st in top of beg ch.

Fasten off.

Finishing

Weave in ends. Felt (see page 144). Slip inner flower into outer flower and sew in place at base.

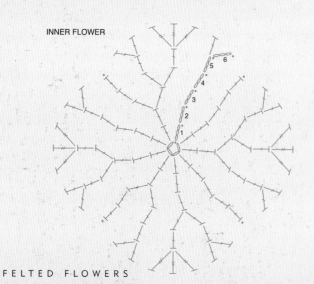

INNER FLOWER

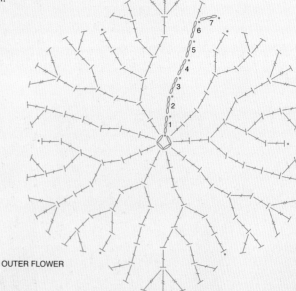

OUTER FLOWER

black and blue flower pin

materials

1 1¾oz/50g ball (each approx 110yd/99m) of Classic Elite Yarns *Renaissance* (wool) in #7191 riviera foam (A) and # 7113 black (B)

Size G/6 (4mm) crochet hook

Three decorative buttons

Pin back

With A, ch 2.

Rnd 1 6 sc in 2nd ch from hook. Join with sl st to first sc.

Rnd 2 Ch 1, 2 sc in each sc around—12 sc. Join with sl st to first sc.

Rnd 3 Ch 1, 2 sc in each sc around—24 sc. Join with sl st to first sc.

Rnd 4 Working in front lps only, *[ch 3, 1 tr] in same st, [2 tr in next st] twice, 1 tr in next st, ch 3, sl st in same st, sl st in next sc; rep from * around, end last rep with sl st in same st—6 petals. Join with sl st in base of beg ch.

Rnd 5 Working in back lps only of rnd 3, sl st in next 2 sts, *[ch 4, dtr] in same st, [2 dtr in next st] twice, 1 dtr in next st, ch 4, sl st in same st, sl st in next sc; rep from * around, end last rep with sl st in same st—6 petals. Join with sl st in base of beg ch-3.

Fasten off A and join B at base of rnd 5 petal.

Rnd 6 Ch 5, *1 sc in top of ch-4 of petal, ch 2, skip 1 dtr, 1 sc in next dtr, ch 3, skip 2 dtr, 1 sc in next dtr, ch2, skip 1 dtr, 1 sc in top of ch-4, ch 3, tr in sp at base of petal, ch 2; rep from * 5 times more, ending last rep 1 sc in top of ch-4, ch 3. Join with sl st in 3rd ch of beg ch-5.

Fasten off.

Felt flower (see page144). When dry, sew buttons to center of flower. Sew or glue pin back to back of flower.

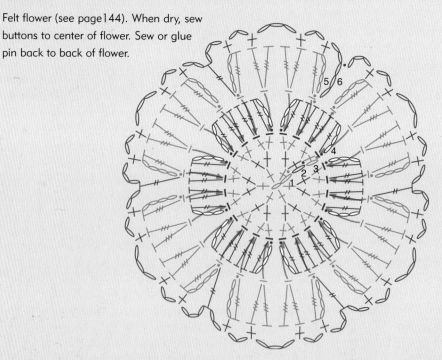

chapter five

chain stitch and ball flowers and leaves

The flowers in this chapter are easy to make, so a project such as the Moonflower Lantern can really be fun to do. The Parisienne scarf is one of my favorites. It can be time-consuming to make because of the small-gauge yarn—but it will be well worth it once you wear it and are showered with compliments! You can also make a shorter version.

Also included here are a variety of leaves that can be used alone or attached to any of the flowers in this book.

leaves

basic leaf (large) • basic leaf (two-color) • basic leaf (small) • oak leaf • classic leaf

materials

1 1¾oz/50g ball (each approx 142yd/130m) of RYC/Westminster Fibers, Inc. *Cashsoft DK* (extrafine wool/microfiber/cashmere) in #523 lichen (A), #509 lime (B), #522 cashew (C) and #515 tape (D)

Size G/6 (4mm) crochet hook

Basic Leaf (large)

With A, ch 14.

Row 1 1 Sl st in 2nd ch from hook, 1 sc in next 3 ch, 1 hdc in next 2 ch, 1 dc in next 3 ch, 2 hdc in next 2 ch, 1 sc in next ch, 3 sc in last ch (working around to other side of foundation ch), 1 sc in next ch, 1 hdc in next 2 ch, 1 dc in next 3 ch, 1 hdc in next 2 ch, 1 sc in next 3 ch, sl st in last ch. Join with sl st to first sl st.

Row 2 Working through back lps only, sl st in each st to 3-sc group, sl st in first sc, ch 2, skip next sc, sl st in 3rd sc, sl st in each st to end. Join with sl st to first sl st and ch 4 for stem.

Fasten off.

Center ridge With RS facing, join A at tip of leaf. Embroider 1 chain st for each ch along foundation ch.

Basic Leaf (two–color)

With B, work Basic Leaf (large) through row 1.

Fasten off B and join A.

With A, work row 2 and center ridge.

Basic Leaf (small)

Leaf

With B, ch 8.

Row 1 1 Sl st in 2nd ch from hook, 1 sc in next ch, 1 hdc in next ch, 1 dc in next ch, 1 hdc in next ch, 1 sc in next ch, 3 sc in last ch (working around to other side of foundation ch), 1 sc in next ch, 1 hdc in next ch, 1 dc in next ch, 1 hdc in next ch, 1 sc in next ch, sl st in last ch. Join with sl st to first sl st.

Row 2 Working through back lps only, sl st in each st to 3-sc group, sl st in first sc, ch 2, skip next sc, sl st in 3rd sc, sl st in each st to end. Join with sl st to first sl st and ch 4 for stem.

Fasten off.

Center ridge With RS facing, join B at tip of leaf. Embroider 1 chain st for each ch along foundation ch.

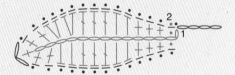

basic leaf (large and two-color)

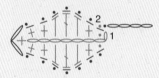

basic leaf (small)

basic leaf (large)

classic leaf

basic leaf
(small)

oak leaf

basic leaf (two- color)

leaves

cont. from previous page

Oak Leaf

With C, ch 2.

Row 1 1 sc in 2nd ch from hook. Turn.

Row 2 Ch 1, 1 sc in sc. Turn.

Row 3 Ch 1, 2 sc in sc. Turn.

Row 4 Ch 1, 2 sc in next 2 sc—4 sc. Turn.

Rows 5–8 Ch 1, 2 sc in first sc, 1 sc in each sc to last sc, 2 sc in last sc—12 sc after row 8. Turn.

Row 9 Ch 1, 1 sc in each sc to end. Turn.

Row 10 Ch 1, 1 hdc in first st, 1 dc in next st, 1 hdc in next st, sl st in next st, 1 sc in next 4 sts, sl st in next st, 1 sc in last 3 sts. Turn.

Row 11 Ch 1, sc2tog, 1 sc in next st, sl st in next st, 1 sc in next 4 sts (leave rem 4 sts unworked). Turn.

Row 12 Ch 1, 1 sc in next 4 sts (leave rem 3 sts unworked). Turn.

Rows 13-16 Ch 1, 2 sc in first sc, 1 sc in each sc to last sc, 2 sc in last sc—12 sc after row 16. Turn.

Rows 17–19 Rep rows 10-12.

Row 20 Ch 1, [sc2tog] twice. Turn.

Row 21 Ch 1, sc2tog.

Fasten off.

Edging

With RS facing, join A at stem end. Ch 1, sc evenly around, working 3 sc at each outside curve and sc2tog at each inside curve. Join with sl st to first sc.

Veins

With A, embroider with chain st as pictured.

oak leaf

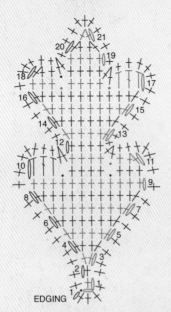

EDGING

Classic Leaf

With D, ch 16.

Row 1 (RS) 1 sc in 2nd ch from hook and in each ch to last ch, 3 sc in last ch (working around to other side of foundation ch), 1 sc in next 14 ch. Do not join. Turn.

Row 2 Working through front lps only, ch 1, 1 sc in next 12 sc (leave rem sts unworked). Turn.

Row 3 Working through back lps only, ch 1, 1 sc in next 11 sc, 3 sc in next sc (working around to other side), 1 sc in next 12 sc (leave rem sts unworked). Turn.

Row 4 Working through front lps only, ch 1, 1 sc in next 11 sc, 3 sc in next sc (working around to other side), 1 sc in next 11 sc (leave rem sts unworked). Turn.

Row 5 Working through back lps only, ch 1, 1 sc in next 10 sc, 3 sc in next sc (working around to other side), 1 sc in next 11 sc (leave rem sts unworked). Turn.

Row 6 Working through front lps only, ch 1, 1 sc in next 11 sc. Join with sl st in next sc. Do not fasten off.

Stem

Ch 20. 1 sc in 2nd ch from hook and in each ch to end. Join with sl st to next sc of leaf. Fasten off.

classic leaf

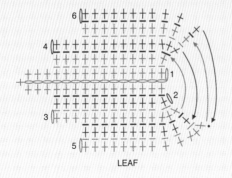

LEAF

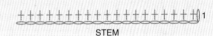

STEM

beaded beauty

materials

1 1¾oz/50g ball (approx 99yd/91m) of Muench *String of Pearls* (cotton/viscose/polyester) in #4004 lime or #4023 turquoise

Size G/6 (4mm) crochet hook

8mm faceted round beads

2mm glass seed beads

Ch 5. Join with sl st in first ch to form a ring.

Rnd 1 Ch 4, 15 tr in ring—16 sts. Join with sl st in top of beg ch.

Rnd 2 *Ch 9, sk next st, sl st in next st; rep from *, end last rep sl st in base of beg ch—8 petals.

Rnd 3 *10 sc in next ch-9 sp, sl st in gap between ch-9 sps; rep from * around.

Fasten off.

Sew beads to center as pictured.

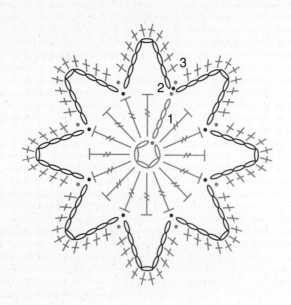

florentines

florentine I • florentine II • florentine III

materials

1 .88oz/25g ball (each approx 115yd/103m) of Jamieson/Simply Shetland 2-ply *Spindrift* in #999 black (A), #587 madder, #577 chestnut (C), and #794 eucalyptus (E)

Size D/3 (3.25mm) crochet hook

Florentine I

With C, ch 2.

Rnd 1 9 sc in 2nd ch from hook. Join with sl st to first sc.

Fasten off C and join D.

Rnd 2 Working in back lps only, ch 1, 2 sc in each sc around—18 sc. Join with sl st to first sc.

Fasten off D and join B.

Rnd 3 Working in front lps only of rnd 2, *ch 7, sl st in next st, ch 7, sk next st, sl st in next st; rep from * around—12 petals.

Fasten off B and join A.

Rnd 4 Working back lps only of rnd 2, ch 3, tr in same st, 2 tr in each st around—36 tr. Join with sl st in beg ch.

Fasten off.

Florentine II

With B, ch 2.

Rnd 1 7 sc in 2nd ch from hook. Join with sl st to first sc.

Fasten off A and join D.

Rnd 2 Working in front lps only, *ch 8, sl st in next st; rep from * around—7 petals.

Fasten off D and join C.

Rnd 3 Working in back lps only of rnd 1, *ch 10, sl st in next st; rep from * around.

Fasten off.

Florentine III

With A, ch 2.

Rnd 1 9 sc in 2nd ch from hook. Join with sl st to first sc.

Fasten off A and join D.

Rnd 2 Working in front lps only, *ch 8, sl st in next st; rep from * around—9 petals.

Fasten off D and join B.

Rnd 3 Working in back lps only of rnd 1, ch 3, tr in same st, 2 tr in each st around —18 tr. Join with sl st in top of beg ch.

Fasten off.

florentine I

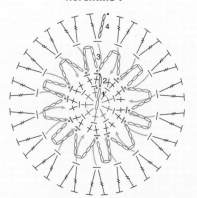

florentine II

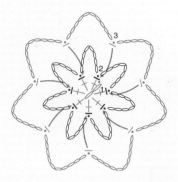

florentine III

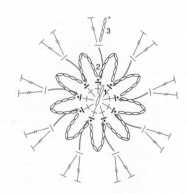

florentine I

florentine III

florentine II

bloomin' balls and floral fantasy

materials

1 1¾oz/50g spool (each approx 145yd/130m) of Fonty/Russi Sales *Serpentine* in #2781 red variegated (A), #840 tomato (B) and #848 mulberry (C)

Size E/4 (3.5mm) crochet hook

Bloomin' Balls

With A, ch 3. Join with sl st in first ch to form a ring.

Rnd 1 Ch 2 (counts as 1 hdc throughout), 7 hdc in ring—8 hdc. Join with sl st in top of beg ch.

Rnd 2 Ch 2, *2 hdc in next hdc, 1 hdc in next hdc; rep from *, end last rep 2 hdc in next hdc—12 hdc. Join with sl st in top of beg ch.

Rnd 3 Ch 2, 1 hdc in each hdc around. Join with sl st in top of beg ch.

Rnd 4 Ch 2, *hdc2tog, 1 hdc in next hdc; rep from *, end last rep hdc2tog—8 hdc. Join with sl st in top of beg ch.

Stuff with filling or waste yarn.

Rnd 5 Ch 2, hdc in next hdc, hdc2tog around—4 hdc. Join with sl st in top of beg ch.

Fasten off.

Using tail, sew opening closed.

Floral Fantasy

Ch 7. Join with sl st in first ch to form a ring.

Rnd 1 Ch 3 (counts as 1 dc), 2 dc in ring, ch 9, *3 dc in ring, ch 9; rep from * 4 times more—6 petals. Join with sl st in top of beg ch.

Rnd 2 Sl st in next dc, ch 1, *1 sc in center dc of 3-dc group, [9 dc, ch 2, 9 dc] in next ch-9 lp, rep from * 5 times more. Join with sl st to first sc. Turn.

Rnd 3 Sl st in first 4 dc, ch 1, *1 sc in next 5 dc, 2 sc in ch-2 sp, 1 sc in next 5 dc, ch 2, skip next 8 dc; rep from * 5 times more. Join with sl st in first sc.

Fasten off.

Sew a Bloomin' Ball at center of flower.

bloomin' balls

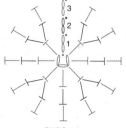

RNDS 1–3

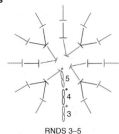

RNDS 3–5

floral fantasy

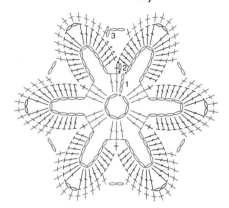

bloomin' balls

floral fantasy

holly

materials

1 1¾oz/50g ball (each approx 103yd/93m) of Tahki Yarns/Tahki•Stacy Charles, Inc. *New Tweed* in #045 green (A), #042 dk red (B) and #050 red (C)

Size F/5 (3.75mm) crochet hook

Small leaf

With A, ch 4.

Row 1 2 sc in 2nd ch from hook, 1 sc in next ch, 2 sc in last ch—5 sc. Turn.

Row 2 Ch 1, [1 sc in first sc, 2 sc in next sc] twice, 1 sc in last sc—7 sc. Turn.

Row 3 Sl st in first 2 sc, 2 sc in next sc, 1 sc in next sc, 2 sc in next sk (leave rem 2 sts unworked)—5 sc. Turn.

Rows 4–7 Rep rnds 2 and 3 twice.

Row 8 Ch 1, sc2tog, sc in next sc, sc2tog—3 sc. Turn.

Row 9 Ch 1, sc3tog.

Fasten off.

Large leaf

With A, ch 11.

Row 1 1 sc in 2nd ch from hook and in each ch to end—10 sc. Turn.

Rows 2 and 4 Ch 1, 1 sc in each sc to end. Turn.

Rows 3 and 5 Ch 1, 1 sc in first sc, 2 sc in next sc, 1 sc in each sc to last 2 sc, 2 sc in next sc, 1 sc in last sc—14 sc after row 5. Turn.

Row 6 Sl st in first 3 sc, ch 1, 1 sc in same st, 1 sc in next 9 sc (leave rem 2 sts unworked)—10 sc. Turn.

Rows 7–11 Rep rows 2–6.

Rows 12–15 Rep rows 2–5.

Row 16 Ch 1, 1 sc in each sc to end. Turn.

Row 17 Sl st in first 4 sc, ch 1, 1 sc in same st, 1 sc in next 5 sc (leave rem 3 sts unworked)—8 sc. Turn.

Row 18 Ch 1, 1 sc in first sc, sc2tog, 1 sc in next 2 sc, sc2tog, 1 sc in last sc—6 sc. Turn.

Row 19 Ch 1, 1 sc in first sc, [sc2tog] twice, 1 sc in last sc—4 sc. Turn.

Row 20 Ch 1, [sc2tog] twice—2 sc. Turn.

Row 21 Ch 1, sc2tog.

Fasten off.

Using tail at chain edge, join beg and end of row 1 to form cup at base of leaf.

Berry

With B or C, ch 4.

[Yo, draw up a lp in 4th ch from hook, yo and draw through 2 lps] 6 times, yo and draw through all 7 lps on hook, ch 1.

Fasten off.

Tie beg and end tails tog to form berry.

Join small leaves at base in pairs and attach berries. Place berries in cupped base of large leaf and sew in place.

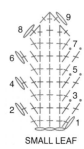

SMALL LEAF

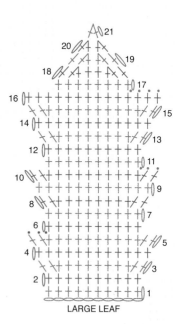

LARGE LEAF

BERRY

moonflower and basic six-petal flower

materials (moonflower)

1 .35oz/10g ball (approx 30yd/27m) of Presencia *Finca* 3 in #3574 dk turquoise

Size D/3 (3.25mm) crochet hook

materials (basic six-petal flower)

1 .35oz/10g ball (approx 30yd/27m) of Presencia *Finca* 3 in #4368 dk emerald

Size D/3 (3.25mm) crochet hook for small flower

Size F/5 (3.75mm) crochet hook for large flower

Moonflower

Version I

Ch 6. Join with sl st in first ch to form a ring.

Rnd 1 Ch 1, 12 sc in ring. Join with sl st in first sc.

Rnd 2 Ch 1, 1 sc in same st, *ch 7, sl st in sc just made, 1 sc in next 2 sc; rep from *, end last rep 1 sc in last sc—6 petals. Join with sl st in first sc.

Rnd 3 Ch 1, *9 sc in ch-7 lp, sl st between next 2 sc; rep from * around.

Join with sl st in sl st of prev rnd.

Rnd 4 Sl st in next 5 st, ch 1, sc in same st, ch 6, *skip next 8 sc, sc in next st, ch 6; rep from * 4 times more. Join with sl st to first sc.

Rnd 5 Ch 1, *8 sc in next ch-6 lp; rep from * around. Join with sl st to first sc.

Fasten off.

Version II

Work same as Version I through rnd 3.

Fasten off.

Basic Six-Petal Flower

Ch 7. Join with sl st in first ch to form a ring.

Rnd 1 Ch 7 (counts as dc, ch 4), *3 dc in ring, ch 4; rep from * 4 times more, 2 dc in ring—6 petals. Join with sl st in top of beg dc.

Rnd 2 Ch 1, *[1 sc, 1 hdc, 1 dc, 3 tr, 1 dc, 1 hdc, 1 sc] in ch-4 sp; rep from * 5 times more. Join with sl st to first sc.

Fasten off.

moonflower

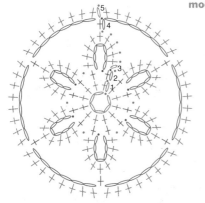

VERSION I

VERSION II

basic six-petal flower

moonflower II

moonflower I

basic six petal flower

queenie, les fleurs and astor

materials

1 .88oz/25g ball (each approx 108yd/97m) of Tahki Yarns/Tahki•Stacy Charles, Inc. *Jolie* in #5020 yellow (A), #5015 blue (B), #5024 dk blue (C), #5016 lt green (D) and #5025 dk green (E)

Size F/5 (3.75mm) crochet hook for small flower

Size G/6 (4mm) crochet hook for large flower

Assorted beads (optional)

Queenie

(make 2 with A, one with each size hook)

Ch 6. Join with sl st in first ch to form a ring.

Rnd 1 Ch 1, 24 sc in ring. Join with sl st to first sc.

Rnd 2 Ch 5 (counts as 1 dc, ch 2), 1 dc in same st, ch 1, skip 2 sts, [(1 dc, ch 2, 1 dc) in next st, ch 1, skip 2 sts] 7 times. Join with sl st in 3rd ch of beg ch-5.

Rnd 3 Ch 2, [1 hdc, ch 2, 2 hdc] in first ch-2 sp, *1 sc in ch-1 sp, [2 hdc, ch 2, 2 hdc] in next ch-2 sp; rep from * 6 times

more 1 sc in ch-1 sp. Join with sl st in top of beg ch.

Fasten off.

Place small flower over large flower and sew in place. Embellish with beads if desired.

Les Fleurs

(make large flower with E, small flower with D)

Ch 6. Join with sl st in first ch to form a ring.

Rnd 1 Ch 1, 14 sc in ring. Join with sl st to first sc.

Rnd 2 Working in front lps only, ch 1 [1 sc, ch 6, 1 sc] in each st around. Join with sl st to first sc.

Rnd 3 Working behind rnd 2 in back lps only of rnd 1, ch 1 [1 sc, ch 8, 1 sc] in each st around. Join with sl st in first sc.

Fasten off.

Place small flower over large flower and sew in place. Sew large round bead at center of flower if desired.

queenie

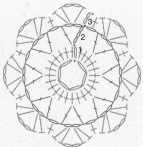

les fleurs

astor

queenie

les fleurs

queenie, les fleurs and astor

cont. from previous page

Astor

(make large flower with B, small flower with C)

Ch 4. Join with sl st in first ch to form a ring.

Rnd 1 Ch 1, 13 sc in ring. Join with sl st to first sc.

Rnd 2 Working in back lps only, *ch 6, sc in 2nd ch from hook and in next 4 ch, sl st in next st; rep from * around—13 petals.

Fasten off B and join C.

Rnd 3 Working in front lps only of rnd 1, ch1, 1 sc in same sp, *ch5, 1 sc in 2nd

ch from hook, 1 hdc in next 2 ch, 1 sc in next ch, 1 sc in next sc of rnd 1; rep from *, end last rep sl st in first sc—13 petals.

Fasten off.

Sew large round bead at center of flower if desired.

astor

wedding lantern trio

materials (flora wedding lantern)

2 2oz/57g balls (each approx 191yd/172m) Coats & Clark *Opera* 5 in #500 white

Size C/2 and D/3 (2.75 and 3.25mm) crochet hooks

One 10" diameter paper lantern

Sewing needle and thread

materials (clover and flower lantern)

3 2oz/57g balls (each approx 191yd/172m) Coats & Clark *Opera* 5 in #500 white

Size C/2 (2.75mm) crochet hook

One 12" diameter paper lantern

Sewing needle and thread

Nine 9mm round pearls

materials (moonflower lantern)

3 2oz/57g balls (each approx 191yd/172m) Coats & Clark *Opera* 5 in #500 white

Size D/3 (3.25mm) crochet hook

One 12" diameter paper lantern

Sewing needle and thread

Spray glue

Flora Wedding Lantern

Flora motif (make 4)

CL3 (3-dc cluster) [Yo and draw up lp, yo and through 2 lps] 3 times in same sp, yo and draw through all 4 lps.

CL3T (3-tr cluster) [Yo twice and draw up lp, (yo and through 2 lps) twice] 3 times in same sp, yo and draw through all 4 lps.

Ch 8. Join with sl st in first ch to form a ring.

Rnd 1 Ch 2, [yo and draw up lp, yo and draw through 2 lps] twice in same sp, yo and draw through all 3 lps, *ch 4, CL3; rep from * 4 times more—6 petals. Join with sl st to first cluster.

Rnd 2 Ch 1, *[1 sc, 1 hdc, 1 dc, 1 tr, 1 dtr, 1 tr, 1 dc, 1 hdc, 1 sc] in next ch-4 sp; rep from * around. Join with sl st to first sc.

Rnd 3 Sl st in next 4 sts (to tip of first petal), *ch 9, sl st in dtr of next petal; rep

wedding lantern trio

cont. from previous page

from * 4 times more, ch 4, tr in dtr of first petal—6 ch-lps.

Rnd 4 Ch 3, [yo twice and draw up lp, (yo and through 2 lps) twice] twice in top of last tr of rnd 3, yo and draw through all 3 lps, ch 4, CL3T in same sp, *ch 6, sl st in sl st at tip of next petal, ch 6, skip 4 ch, [CL3T, ch 4, CL3T] in next ch; rep from * 4 times more, ch 6, sl st in tip of last petal, ch 6. Join with sl st to first cluster.

Rnd 5 Ch 1, *[3 sc, ch 3, sl st in previous sc, 3 sc] in ch-4 sp, sl st in next cluster, ch 10, sl st in next cluster; rep from * 4 times more, [3 sc, ch 3, sl st in previous sc, 3 sc] in last ch-4 sp, sl st in next cluster, ch 5,

CL3T in next sl st, ch 5. Join with sl st to first sc.

Fasten off.

Top border

Ch 120. Join with sl st in first ch to form a ring.

Rnd 1 Ch 1, *2 sc in first ch, 1 sc in next 4 ch; rep from * to end—144 sc. Join with sl st to first sc.

Rnd 2 Ch 3 (counts as 1 dc), 1 dc in next sc and in each sc around. Join with sl st in top of beg ch.

Rnd 3 Ch 1, 1 sc in each dc around. Join with sl st to first sc.

Rnd 4 Ch 5 (counts as 1 dc, ch 2), *skip 2 sc, 1 dc in next sc, ch 2; rep from * around—48 ch-2 sp. Join with sl st in 3rd ch of beg ch-5.

Netting

Rnd 5 Ch 1, *1 sc in ch-2 sp, ch 6, skip next 2dc; rep from * around—24 ch-6 lps. Join with sl st to first sc.

Rnd 6 Sl st in next 3 ch, ch 1, *1 sc in ch-6 lp, ch 10; rep from * around—24 ch-10 lps. Join with sl st to first sc.

Rnds 7, 8 and 9 Sl st in next 5 ch, ch 1, *1 sc in ch-10 lp, ch 10; rep from * around. Join with sl st to first sc.

flora wedding lantern

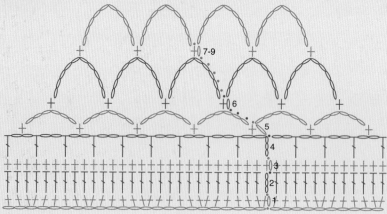

TOP BORDER

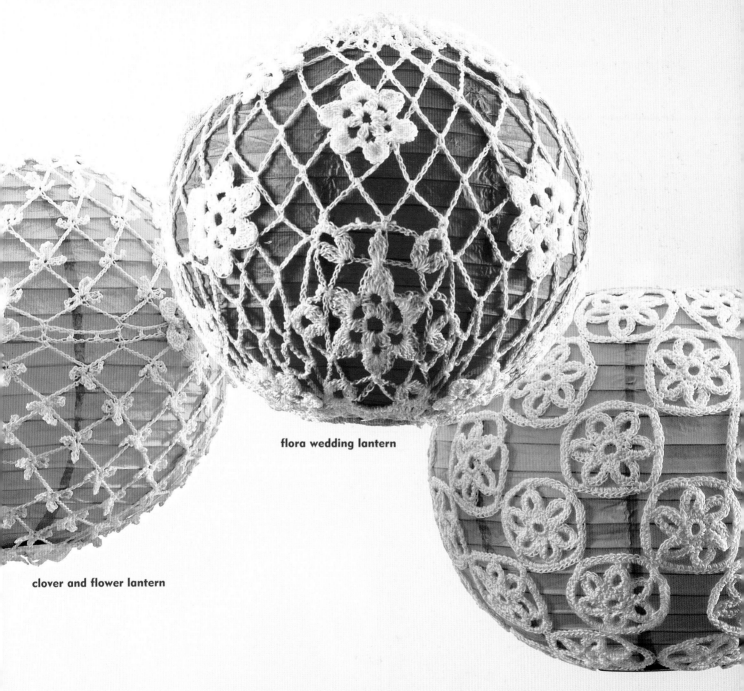

clover and flower lantern

flora wedding lantern

moonflower lantern

wedding lantern trio

cont. from previous page

Fasten off.

Join motifs to top border

Join thread to any ch-10 lp in last rnd of top border.

Rnd 1 *Ch 5, join first motif at ch-3 picot with sl st, ch 5, 1 sc in ch-10 lp of top border, ch 5, join motif at CL3T with sl st, ch 5, 1 sc in ch-10 lp of top border, ch 5, join motif at ch-3 picot with sl st, ch 5, 1 sc in ch-10 lp of top border, [ch 10, 1 sc in ch-10 lp of top border] 3 times; rep from * 3 times more, end last rep [ch 10, 1 sc in ch-10 lp] twice, ch 10. Join with sl st in base of beg ch-5.

Fasten off.

Filler

Working between motifs, join thread to RH motif in 3rd sc above joined picot.

Row 1 Ch 5, 1 sc in ch-10 lp, [ch 10, 1 sc in ch-10 lp] twice, ch 5, sl st in 3rd sc above joined picot. Turn.

Row 2 [Ch 10, 1 sc in ch-10 lp] twice, ch 10, sl st in sc where thread was joined. Fasten off.

Rejoin thread at picot above previous join.

Row 3 Ch 5, 1 sc in ch-10 lp, [ch 10, 1 sc in ch-10 lp] twice, ch 5, sl st in corresponding picot of LH motif. Turn.

Row 4 [Ch 10, 1 sc in ch-10 lp] twice, ch 10, sl st in picot where thread was joined. Fasten off.

Rejoin thread in ch-10 lp above previous picot.

Row 5 [Ch 10, 1 sc in ch-10 lp] 3 times, ch 10, sl st in ch-10 lp above picot, ch 5, sl st in next picot of same motif. Turn.

Row 6 [Ch 5, 1 sc in ch-10 lp] 4 times, ch 5, sl st in picot above join. Fasten off.

Rep rows 1–6 in rem 3 spaces. Do not fasten off after last space. Turn.

Bottom border

Rnd 1 Ch 3, *[1 dc in next ch, (skip 1 ch, 1 dc in next ch) twice] 5 times, 1 dc in next 3 sc, [skip 1 ch, 1 dc in next ch] 5 times, 1 dc in next 3 sc; rep from * 3 times more. Join with sl st in top of beg ch.

Rnd 2 Ch 1, 1 sc in each dc around. Join with sl st to first sc.

Rnd 3 Ch 1, 1 sc in each sc around. Join with sl st to first sc.

Finishing

Flowers

Make 12 with smaller hook and 4 with larger hook.

Work rnds 1 and 2 of motif. Fasten off.

Sew 2 rows of 4 smaller flowers around upper half of netting and 1 row of 4 smaller flowers around lower border. Sew 4 larger flowers between top edges of motifs.

Using 2 lengths of thread held together, thread through dc rnd at top and bottom borders and draw closed to size of openings. Knot and weave in ends.

flora wedding lantern

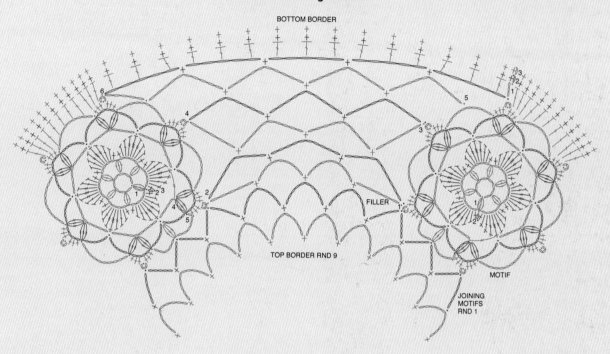

BOTTOM BORDER

MOTIF

FILLER

TOP BORDER RND 9

JOINING
MOTIFS
RND 1

flora wedding lantern

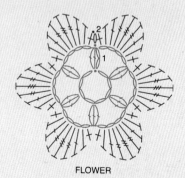

FLOWER

wedding lantern trio

cont. from previous page

Clover and Flower Lantern

First half

Ch 180. Join with sl st in first ch to form a ring.

Rnd 1 Ch 5, *skip 2 ch, 1 dc in next ch, ch 2; rep from *, end skip 2 ch—60 ch-2 sp. Join with sl st in 3rd ch of beg ch-5.

Rnd 2 *Ch 6, [ch 7, sl st in 7th ch from hook] 3 times, sl st in 6th ch of previous ch-6, ch 6, skip next 2 dc, 1 sc in next dc; rep from *, end last rep skip last 2 dc–20 clovers. Join with sl st in base of beg ch.

Rnd 3 Sl st in next 6 ch, * working behind petals; 1 sc between first 2 petals of clover, ch 1, 1 sc between last 2 petals of clover,

ch 6, [ch 7, sl st in 7th ch from hook] 3 times, sl st in 6th ch of previous ch-6, ch 6; rep from * around. Join with sl st to first sc.

Rnd 4 Sl st in next ch-sp, sl st in next 6 ch, * working behind petals 1 sc bet first 2 petals of clover, ch 1, 1 sc bet last 2 petals of clover, ch 6, [ch 7, sl st in 7th ch from hook] 3 times, sl st in 6th ch of previous ch-6, ch 6; rep from * around. Join with sl st to first sc.

Rnds 5–8 Rep rnd 4.

Fasten off.

Second half

Join yarn to joining sl st of foundation ch.

Rep rnds 2–8 of first half, working rnd 2 in base of dc along foundation ch.

Fasten off.

Flower (make 9)

CL4 [Yo and draw up lp, yo and through 2 lps] 4 times in same sp, yo and draw through all 5 lps.

Ch 6. Join with sl st in first ch to form a ring.

Rnd 1 Ch 3, [yo and draw up lp, yo and draw through 2 lps] 3 times, yo and draw through all 4 lps, *ch 4, CL4; rep from * 4 times more, ch 4—6 petals. Join with sl st to first cluster.

clover and flower lantern

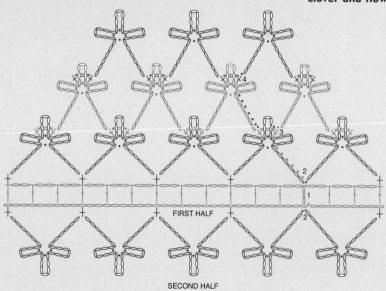

FIRST HALF

SECOND HALF

FLOWER

Rnd 2 Ch 1, *[1 sc, 1 hdc, 1 dc, 2 tr, 1 dc, 1 hdc, 1 sc] in next ch-4 sp; rep from * around. Join with sl st in first sc.

Fasten off.

Finishing

Make two 12"/30.5cm chains. Slip cover over lantern. Thread one chain each through center petals at top and bottom and gather to close. Sew a pearl to center of each flower, and attach flowers evenly around center band (rnd 1 of first half).

Moonflower Lantern

Moonflower (make 52)

Ch 6. Join with sl st in first ch to form a ring.

Rnd 1 Ch 1, 12 sc in ring. Join with sl st to first sc.

Rnd 2 Ch 1, 1 sc in same st, *ch 7, sl st in previous sc, 1 sc in next 2 sc; rep from * 4 times more, ch 7, sl st in prevous sc, 1 sc in last sc—6 ch-7 lps. Join with sl st to first sc.

Rnd 3 Ch 1, *9 sc in next ch-7 lp, sl st between 2 sc; rep from * around.

Rnd 4 Sl st in next 5 sc, ch 1, 1 sc in same sc (center sc of 9-sc petal), ch 7, *skip next 8 sc, 1 sc in next sc, ch 7; rep from * 4 times more. Join with sl st to first sc.

Rnd 5 Ch 1, *8 sc in next ch-7 sp; rep from * 5 times more. Join with sl st to first sc.

Fasten off.

Assembly

When assembling the flowers on the lantern, it helps to first spray the lantern with a light coating of spray glue. The flowers will then adhere to the lantern as you sew them together.

Top ring Join yarn to first motif at beg of one 8-sc group. Ch 1, *1 sc in next 8 sc, ch 1; rep from * in next motif 8 times more. Join with sl st to first sc to form a ring of 9 motifs. Fasten off. Place around top opening of lantern.

Body With needle and thread, attach 4 rows of flowers (8/9/9/8 motifs), staggering each row as pictured and tacking motifs to each other as you go.

Bottom ring Attach remaining 9 flowers around bottom opening. Sc around bottom opening as for top ring.

moonflower lantern

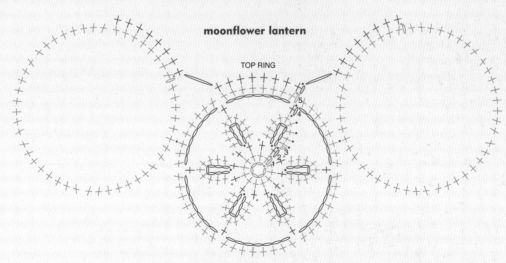

TOP RING

parisienne scarf

size

Approx 9"W x 72"L/23cm x 183cm

materials

20 .88oz/25g balls (each approx 230yd/210m) of Rowan/Westminster Fibers, Inc. *Kidsilk Haze* (kid mohair/silk) in assorted colors

Size D/3 (3.25mm) crochet hook

Tapestry needle

note

Choice of yarn colors is designated by letters for each circle motif.

Make 120 circles as foll: 60 large and 60 small, in any combination of colors.

Large circle

With A, ch 2.

Rnd 1 With A, 9 sc in first ch. Join with sl st to first sc.

Fasten off A and join B.

Rnd 2 With B, ch 2 (counts as 1 dc), 1 dc in same sc, 2 dc in each sc around—18 dc. Join with sl st in top of beg ch-2.

Fasten off B and join C.

Rnd 3 With C, ch 2, 1 dc in each dc around. Join with sl st in top of beg ch-2.

Fasten off C.

Rnd 4 With D, ch 1, 1 sc in first and in each dc around. Join with sl st to first sc.

Small circle

With A, ch 2.

Rnd 1 With A, 9 sc in first ch. Join with sl st to first sc.

Fasten off A and join B.

Rnd 2 With B, ch 1, 2 sc in each sc around—18 sc. Join with sl st to first sc.

Fasten off B and join C.

Rnd 3 With C, ch 2, 1 dc in each sc around. Join with sl st in top of beg ch-2.

Fasten off.

Chain petal

Note Work randomly on as many or few circles as desired.

Join B to any st of rnd 2.

*Ch 5, sl st around post of next st of rnd 2; rep from * around. Join with sl st to first ch of beg ch-5.

Finishing

With WS facing up, lay out circles in 4 columns of 30 each, alternating large and small circles. With tapestry needle and 1 strand of yarn, stitch circles together at edges where they touch.

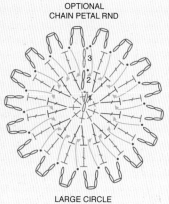

OPTIONAL
CHAIN PETAL RND

LARGE CIRCLE
RNDS 1–3

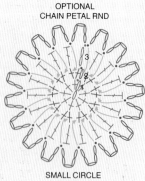

OPTIONAL
CHAIN PETAL RND

SMALL CIRCLE
RNDS 1–3

glamour gloves

gauge

1 flower = 1½"/4cm diameter

materials

1 1¾oz/50g spool (each approx 145yd/130m) of Fonty/Russi Sales *Serpentine* in #825 black (A) and #848 mulberry (B)

Size D/3 (3.25mm) crochet hook

Ten 7mm faceted glass beads in black

Purchased opera gloves

Sewing needle and matching thread

Make 10 flowers.

With A, ch 2.

Rnd 1 7 sc in 2nd ch from hook. Join with sl st to first sc.

Fasten off A and join B.

Rnd 2 Working in front lps only, *ch 10, sl st in next st; rep from * around.

Fasten off.

Finishing

Sew bead to center of each flower. For each glove, position 5 flowers evenly spaced from wrist to opening and sew in place.

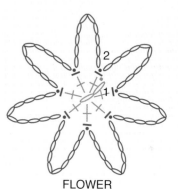

FLOWER

florette pillow

materials

1 3½oz/100g ball (each approx 207yd/188m) of Lion Brand Yarn *Cotton-Ease* in #099 almond (A), #149 stone (A), #152 charcoal (B) and #122 taupe (B)

Size G/6 (4mm) crochet hook

One round gusseted pillow 18"/45.5cm diameter and 3"/7.5cm thick

Sewing needle and matching thread

note

Adjust number of flowers for different-sized pillows.

Flower

Make 60, alternating yarns A for rnds 1 and 2 and yarns B for rnd 2.

With A, ch 4. Join with sl st in first ch to form a ring.

Rnd 1 Ch 1, 11 sc in ring. Join with sl st to first sc.

Rnd 2 Working in front lps only, ch 1 [1 sc, ch 4, 1 sc] in each sc around—11 petals. Join with sl st to first sc.

Fasten off A and join B in back lp of any sc of rnd 1.

Rnd 3 Working in back lps only of rnd 1, ch 1, [1 sc, ch 6, 1 sc] in each sc around —11 petals. Join with sl st to first sc.

Fasten off.

Using sewing needle and thread, sew flowers to pillow as pictured.

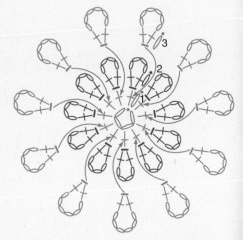

techniques

Felting

Fill washing machine to low water setting at a hot temperature. Add ¼ cup of a gentle detergent. Add all pieces and a pair of jeans to provide abrasion and balanced agitation. Use a 15–20 minute wash cycle, including cold rinse and spin. Check measurements of piece. If it is still larger than finished measurements, repeat process with progressively shorter cycles, measuring every few minutes until measurement is achieved. Form piece into shape. Let air dry.

Felting by hand is more labor-intensive than felting by machine, but it wastes less water, particularly when you are felting a swatch or a small project.

Soak the finished item in hot water for 30 minutes or until it is completely saturated. Add a small amount of soap. Agitate the piece by rubbing and kneading. This may take some time, so be patient.

If the water cools, add more hot water.

When the fibers are matted and you don't want the item to shrink any more, rinse it in tepid water. Roll item in a towel and squeeze out excess water. Do NOT wring—it may pull the item out of shape!

resources

Alchemy Yarns of Transformation
P.O. Box 1080
Sebastopol, CA 95473
707.823.3276
www.alchemyyarns.com

Artyarns, Inc.
39 Westmoreland Avenue
White Plains, NY 10606
www.artyarns.com

Classic Elite Yarns
122 Western Avenue
Lowell, MA 01851
www.classiceliteyarns.com

Coats & Clark
3430 Toringdon Way, Suite 301
Charlotte, NC 28277
www.coatsandclark.com

DMC
#10F Port Kearny, South Hackensack
Avenue
South Kearny, NJ 07302
www.dmc.com

Filatura Di Crosa
Distributed by Tahki•Stacy Charles, Inc.

Fonty
Distributed by Russi Sales

GGH
Distributed by Muench Yarns

Jamieson's/Simply Shetland
10 Domingo Road
Santa Fe, NM 87508
www.simplyshetland.net

Koigu Wool Designs
Box 158
563295 Glenelg Holland Townline
Chatsworth, Ontario N0H 1G0
Canada
www.koigu.com

Lane Borgosesia
Distributed by Trendsetter Yarns

Lion Brand Yarn
34 West 15th Street
New York, NY 10011
www.lionbrand.com

Lorna's Laces
4229 North Honore Street
Chicago, IL 60613
www.lornaslaces.net

Muench Yarns
1323 Scott Street
Petaluma, CA 94954
www.muenchyarns.com

Nashua Handknits
Distributed by Westminster Fibers, Inc.

Presencia
P.O. Box 2409
Evergreen, CO 80437
www.presenciausa.com

Rowan Yarns
Distributed by Westminster Fibers, Inc.
In the U.K.: Green Lane Mill
Holmfirth
HD9 2DX England
www.knitrowan.com

Russi Sales
605 Clark Road
Bellingham, WA 98225
www.russisales.com

RYC
Distributed by Westminster Fibers, Inc.

S. Charles Collezione
Distributed by Tahki•Stacy Charles, Inc.

Tahki Yarns
Distributed by Tahki•Stacy Charles, Inc.

Tahki•Stacy Charles, Inc.
70-30 80th Street
Building #36
Ridgewood, NY 11385
www.tahkistacycharles.com

Tilli Tomas
72 Woodland Road
Boston, MA 02130
www.tillitomas.com

Trendsetter Yarns
16745 Saticoy Street #101
Van Nuys, CA 91406
www.trendsetter.com

Westminster Fibers
165 Ledge Street
Nashua, NH 03060
www.westminsterfibers.com

acknowledgments

Many thanks to my intrepid crocheters Jo Brandon, Eileen Curry and Nancy Henderson, and to Margaret Hubert for her sweet encouragement.

Thanks to my masterful art director, Chi Ling Moy, who created the beautiful garden for my flowers to grow in, and to the lovely photography of Jennifer Lévy that captured the essence and detail of the pieces.

As always, thanks to the staff of Sixth&Spring Books, led by Trisha Malcolm, who continue to encourage and support me in so many ways. They include Elaine Silverstein, Erica Smith, Sheena T. Paul and Tanis Gray. Thanks also to Eve Ng, Karen Manthey and Jeannie Chin for turning their keen eyes to the instructions and charts.

And finally, thanks to my many loyal crochet friends and fans who continue to remind me that knitting is not the only needlecraft art!

INDEX

INDEX